Mary Seymour

Story of the Life of Saint Paul the Apostle

Mary Seymour

Story of the Life of Saint Paul the Apostle

ISBN/EAN: 9783337573102

Printed in Europe, USA, Canada, Australia, Japan

Cover: Foto ©Lupo / pixelio.de

More available books at **www.hansebooks.com**

STORY OF

THE LIFE OF ST. PAUL,

THE APOSTLE.

By M. F. S.,

AUTHOR OF "LEGENDS OF THE SAINTS,"
"STORIES OF THE SAINTS," "STORIES OF MARTYR PRIESTS," "TOM'S
CRUCIFIX AND OTHER TALES," "CATHERINE HAMILTON,"
"CATHERINE GROWN OLDER," "THE THREE WISHES," &c.

London:
R. WASHBOURNE, 18 PATERNOSTER ROW.
1877.

TO

**THE FATHERS OF THE SACRED HEART
FOR FOREIGN MISSIONS,**

WHO,

OBEYING THEIR VOCATION,

ARE DEVOTING THEIR LIVES

TO THE APOSTLESHIP

OF

HEATHEN PEOPLE,

THIS STORY OF THE LIFE

OF THE GREAT APOSTLE

OF NATIONS

IS

𝔇𝔢𝔡𝔦𝔠𝔞𝔱𝔢𝔡.

PREFACE.

Of all the Christians that have ever lived, there is, perhaps, not one whose life is invested with a greater interest than that of St. Paul the Apostle. A Jew of the tribe of Benjamin, of the strictest sect of the Pharisees, highly educated, and brought up under the eye of the chief doctor and teacher of that time, a man of position among the Jews, he must necessarily have been one of the most conspicuous of the early converts to Christianity; even had his conversion not been miraculous. But to us Gentile Christians, St. Paul, the Hebrew of the Hebrews, stands in a very special relation; for he, as the Apostle of the Gentiles, reminds us that we have a claim to the promises which God made to Abraham —promises which the parenthetical dispensation of the Law could in no way disannul. It is in his writings especially that we read of the liberty of Christians, and of the necessity, power, and abundance of the grace of God; of the personal relation to God in which all true religion consists; of conscience, which makes the just man a law to himself; and of a simple interior godliness which he speaks of as Christ being formed in us.

But while he insists on our spiritual freedom, he dwells no less strongly on our duties—on the sincere charity that we owe one to another; the care we should take to avoid scandal; the interior preparation with which we should approach the holy sacraments; and the truth and reality that should pervade our lives.

St. Paul, too, is a great example and teacher of the way in which we should conduct ourselves towards unbelievers and the civil law of the State. For we find him not only showing charity to all men, and respect and submission to the magistrates and rulers in all that was lawful, but also availing himself of all his civil rights and privileges as a Roman citizen.

And does not the condition of our own times increase and intensify the interest which must alway attach to the life of this great Apostle? The wide-spread structure of mediæval Christendom is broken up, and public opinion is no longer on the side of right because right is the Will of God. Nations frame laws and constitutions which recognise neither the Church, nor the God Who founded it.

As it was in the days of St. Paul, so is it now: material prosperity, luxury, and pleasure, are the ends for which men live. The Church, now as then, is a private community of believers, depending, after the grace of God, on the good-will of its members individually, and on no authority derived from civil governments; indeed, there is hardly a nation upon earth in which the Church is even free, unless it be ignored. Those that are without look upon it now with much the same feelings of fear, wonder, hatred, or contempt as men regarded it in the days of the Apostles. Many a Gallio lives now indifferent to all religions; many a Demetrius who judges of religion simply by the gain it brings to the craftsmen; many an Agrippa who is all but a Christian; many a polished Nero ready to persecute.

Meanwhile, we that are within are cheered by the same hopes, and tried by many of the same temptations, as were the lot of the early Christians.

May the great Apostle of the Gentiles

guide and help us in times which are growing more and more like to his own, and obtain by his prayers that Christ may live in us by grace, and truth, and peace.

W. J. B. R.

January, 1877.

STORY OF THE
LIFE OF ST. PAUL,
THE APOSTLE.

CHAPTER I.

A YEAR had scarcely passed after the death of Christ, when a young man of honourable birth and great learning visited the city of Jerusalem at the time of the religious festivals, and there discovered that people of every rank were being attracted to a new faith—the faith which Jesus had taught from His own lips while He dwelt on earth, and which His Apostles were now preaching in the midst of danger, difficulty, and unbelief. Saul was filled with the fiercest indignation. His father was a Pharisee who had carefully trained his son in their strict and austere rules. From his earliest years he had been instructed in the laws and traditions of the Jews by Gamaliel, the most noted teacher of that day, and he had far excelled his companions in the acquirement of that knowledge which was so highly valued by the sect to which he belonged; and now, in his first anger and hot zeal, the young man believed it his duty and his glory to root out the Christian truth which *he* deemed heresy, and to destroy all who avowed themselves followers of Jesus of Nazareth.

Tarsus, in Cilicia, was Saul's native city, and he must have been dwelling there during the period of our Lord's public ministry, for no record exists of his having witnessed any of the wondrous scenes connected with the life and death of Christ; and it is supposed that, after completing his studies at Jerusalem, he returned to his home, remaining there until the year 35, when his career of persecuting cruelty began by the martyrdom of St. Stephen, about the time of the Feast of Pentecost. The Scripture narrative does not mention Saul's name as one of those who took Stephen captive, but probably he was among the number who listened to that speech before the council, when we are told that the martyr's face was "as the face of an angel."

It is at the scene of the stoning that we hear of Saul—the young man at whose feet the witnesses laid down their garments, thus choosing him for their commander and chief; and when the dying Saint cried, "Lord Jesus, receive my spirit," and, "Lord, lay not this sin to their charge," Saul was there, consenting to his death.

Little did the fierce and angry multitude think of the marvels which St. Stephen's dying prayer would work, pleading effectually with God, and securing the conversion of the young man Saul, who was then one of the most bitter enemies of the Christian Church. Perhaps, in those last moments, it was permitted the martyred Saint to understand in some measure some of the purposes of the Almighty in his sufferings and death—to know, maybe, that very near him, in the ranks of the cruel and persecuting throng, stood the man who had been chosen as the agent to carry out the gracious designs of Providence towards the Gentile world.

However, the stoning of the Protomartyr was followed for some considerable time by a course of merciless severity. Saul scourged, imprisoned, and put to death, men and women to whom the name of Christ was dearer than aught else, even than life; driving them by thousands from Jerusalem, and even pursuing them into their hiding-places, that he might force them back to die.

Thus it came about that Saul was journeying to Damascus.

It was well known that many of the persecuted Christians had sought refuge in that city, and Saul, "breathing out threatenings and slaughter against the disciples of the Lord," went to the high priest to obtain from him authority to seize all who were known to be believers in the new faith, and to bring them back to Jerusalem.

His journey was almost accomplished. Already the walls of the then beautiful city were within his sight; his heart beat high with triumph, when suddenly he was stayed, and, swifter than gleam of lightning, an unnatural brilliancy encompassed Saul and his attendants, who, confused and dazzled, fell prostrate on the ground.

A voice from heaven was heard—not in tones of anger or reproach, to terrify the bold persecutor of Christians, but sweetly, softly, sorrowfully it sounded in his ear, speaking words which none but he could understand—

"Saul, Saul, why persecutest thou Me?"

Oh, wondrous power of the gentleness of Jesus! The haughty Pharisee became in that brief moment humble and yielding as a little child, and answered, "Who art thou, Lord?"

"I am Jesus whom thou persecutest," said the heavenly voice.

Those who were with Saul heard not these words, nor was it permitted them to see Christ. They were only conscious of the overwhelming brilliancy of the flood of light, and knew too that a strange voice seemed speaking—the privilege of beholding in vision the Saviour of the world was reserved for the man who had so deeply grieved Him.

"Lord, what wouldst Thou have me to do?" inquired the now humbled Pharisee, and the answer came at once—

"Go into the city, and there it shall be told thee what thou shalt do."

It was a hard and humiliating command to one like Saul!

He—so well versed in classical learning, honoured for his superior attainments, followed by numbers who trusted implicitly in his wise counsels—must he indeed in submissive obedience learn from the lips of man what was the Will of God?

Was it not also harder still to hear that he should be required to teach the very faith he had openly despised to the Gentiles, for whom, as a Pharisee, he had the deepest contempt and scorn?

It *was* hard to human nature, but Divine grace was strong, and Saul did not hesitate, but suffered his attendants to lead him to Damascus, still blind from the effect of the wondrous light which had shone upon and around him, there to do whatever God should direct.

In the grand old city, in a street called "Straight," which is said still to exist, there dwelt near the eastern gate a man named Judas, who received Saul into his house. While staying there, a vision was granted to the sufferer, promising him relief, and naming a Christian man of that city who should speedily come and visit him.

This man was Ananias, who also was directed from heaven to seek out Saul of Tarsus, the well-known persecutor of Christians.

That name had a terror for the servants of God in Damascus, and Ananias was alarmed.

"Behold, he prays," the voice had said, and yet the Christian hesitated, for he knew full well that Saul had received from the high priest authority to bind all who were followers of Jesus.

But the command, "Go thy way," stayed his many doubts, and, confiding in God's care, Ananias set out for the house of Judas.

Arriving there, he laid his hand on Saul, saying that God had sent him that he might receive once more his sight and be filled with the Holy Ghost; and at once, by the power of the Almighty, he was blind no longer, and, by the direction of Ananias, he received baptism, and avowed himself from henceforth to be among the followers of Christ.

Having recovered his strength, Saul entered the Jewish synagogue in Damascus to proclaim the message of the Son of God whom he had before rejected and despised, and the people there asked each other in amazement if this could be he who had come to the city as the enemy of Christians.

Their surprise served only to animate Saul with still greater zeal in preaching that the promised Messiah, so long expected, had really dwelt upon the earth in the person of Jesus of Nazareth, the crucified God.

Shortly after his conversion, Saul travelled into the desert regions of Arabia, to fit himself by prayer and solitude for his future work; to learn those lessons of self-knowledge and self-distrust, without which no active work can be done for God's sole glory; and —separated from the business of this world—to hold communion with his Creator.

Three years of silence and retirement—years in which the once well-known Pharisee was almost forgotten by the crowd who had followed him in his old days of influence and power—and then Saul came forth to do his Master's work imbued with those deep principles of spiritual life which should sustain and guide him in the arduous labours which he was about to undertake on his return to Damascus, and the Jewish people there.

But just as fiercely, just as deeply as Saul had once hated the holy Stephen, so did the Jews in the city hate and resolve to destroy him.

A plot was laid for his apprehension, and three men were stationed at the different gates of Damascus in order to slay him if he should try to escape; but his friends placed him in one of the large, strong baskets common in the East, and let him down by ropes from the window of a house close to the city wall; and thus freed he made his way to Jerusalem. Arrived there, Saul asked eagerly for the disciples of Jesus, but they were afraid that he only sought to betray them; for, although three years had passed since his conversion, it had not become known in Jerusalem, and neither St. Peter nor St. James, who were there, believed that Saul was a Christian.

It was a fresh humiliation for that proud, lofty nature to be thus mistrusted and rejected by Christ's own Apostles, but it served to deepen his contrition for his former bitter persecution of the Church. One friend was raised up for him in St. Barnabas, who, remembering the honour and distinction which had attended Saul's departure from Jerusalem, pitied him in this humiliating return, and undertook to make known the wonderful story of his change of heart to the other Apostles.

Hearing this, they were no longer fearful, but welcomed Saul as one of their brethren, and gladly permitted him to share in their work, so that he at once began to labour for the conversion of the Grecian Jews in the city.

But they remembered him as one of their own party, one whom they had honoured as a Pharisee, and who had been their leader in the work of persecution; and these facts made them so much the more bitter in their hatred, and they began to conspire against his life.

One day, while Saul prayed in the temple, he fell into that strange supernatural state of ecstasy in which the prophets of old, and the Apostles and Saints of later times, have received messages and revelations from Heaven. It was the Lord Jesus Christ Who thus in vision appeared to His servant, bidding him leave Jerusalem because the Jews there would not receive his words, and declaring it to be the Divine purpose that he should journey afar off—to the Gentiles.

Doubtless, in the freshness and fervour of his newly-felt love, Saul would have chosen rather to remain in the city and give up his life for God, but with that great faith and ready submission of will which grace had implanted in his heart, he yielded without hesitation; and, going down to Cæsarea, entered a ship bound for Syria, and made his way to Tarsus, where he remained for many years. During that time Saul's life was secluded, and very few positive records of it remain; but it was then he took short voyages to the different towns on the coast, and suffered the shipwrecks which are mentioned in his Epistles to the Corinthians. There, too, he endured some of that hunger and thirst, scourging and imprisonment, which he suffered for the sake of Christ, and received, as it is believed, many of those wonderful revelations which God granted as a help and consolation in his trials, as well as in preparation for the still greater difficulties which were hidden in the future.

All this time the Jews, who were still unbelievers, pursued Saul with the deepest hatred and longing for revenge.

He had forfeited his patrimony on

becoming one of the sect of Christians, and he had then no Gentile friends to help and to pity him, yet he was content; for, as he tells us in his Epistle to the Philippians, he esteemed "all things to be but loss for the excellent knowledge of Jesus Christ, my Lord."

Meanwhile, St. Peter had visited the different towns and villages, and at length, reaching Joppa, took up his abode in the house of a man named Simon, by trade a tanner.

There, one day at noontide, as he reclined in Eastern fashion upon the housetop, he turned his heart to God, and, forgetting all earthly things, became absorbed in contemplation.

A feeling of intense, supernatural hunger came upon him then, and as his friends prepared food, he fell into a rapture, and saw the heavens open, and a sheet descend which contained animals of every description.

St. Peter had the strong Jewish regard for the distinctions of the law concerning the clean and the unclean, therefore when a voice directed him to kill and eat of these animals, he answered, "Far be it from me, for I never did eat anything that is common or unclean."

A second time the voice spoke to him. "That which God hath cleansed do not thou call common," it said; and when this mysterious vision had been three times repeated, the sheet was drawn up to heaven again.

In the same manner that the Jews avoided eating such food as the old ceremonial law of Moses deemed unclean, so they shunned all intercourse with the Gentiles as an unclean nation.

This remarkable vision was God's way of teaching St. Peter that the prejudices of his life must be laid aside, and as fully as grace was poured out upon the Gentile world, so he must also admit them to all the blessings of the Christian Church.

While St. Peter pondered over this wondrous revelation of God's Will, two servants and a soldier came to the tanner's house, and asked if one Simon, surnamed Peter, was lodging there.

They came from Cornelius, an officer in the Roman army, who dwelt in Cæsarea, a fine city and seaport some thirty-five miles from Joppa. We read in Scripture that Cornelius was a devout man, and that he gave alms to the people, and spent much time in prayer. He must, therefore, have been conscientiously following the light he had, and praying to know God's Will; and such humble constant prayer can never be disregarded by Heaven. So it happened that one evening as Cornelius prayed, a heavenly visitor appeared to him, speaking in gentle tones of love, and yet he was alarmed, and exclaimed, "What is it, Lord?"

Then he heard that his prayers and his alms had gone up as a memorial before the throne of God, and he was bidden to send men to Joppa, who should bring to him Peter, then lodging with a tanner in his humble dwelling upon the sea-shore.

We have already seen these messengers reaching the dwelling of the Apostle; and while they asked for him, the Holy Spirit made their arrival known to St. Peter, and inspired him to go with them, for it was God Who sent them.

Immediately leaving the housetop, the Apostle went to the door, and heard how the messengers had come from Cornelius, and also that he had been directed by an angel to send to Joppa.

Strong though his Jewish prejudices had been, love of his Master's will and his Master's work were still stronger, and St. Peter made the Gentile visitors welcome for the night, and departed with them next day for Cæsarea, taking with him some of his Christian brethren.

When they reached the house of Cornelius, they found him with his friends, assembled to receive the much-desired visitor; and meeting St. Peter at the portico of his house, he prostrated himself with the greatest reverence and humility, recognising the Apostle as the visible head of the

Christian Church, and the representative of Jesus Christ.

St. Peter raised him from the ground, and entering the house, began speaking of the old Jewish law which had prohibited intercourse with other nations, telling his hearers that God now commanded all those restrictions to end, and therefore he came among them as readily as if they were his own Jewish brethren.

Cornelius then related the favour which had been granted him, and said that they were all there assembled to hear the words of life from the lips of the Apostle.

St. Peter now tells the glad news of Christ's coming amongst men. He tells them that the once despised and outcast Gentiles are not only invited to receive God's grace, but are to be in all things equal partakers with the Jewish people—that Christ, of Whose resurrection and ascension they had already heard, had given an express commission to His Apostles to preach the Gospel to all nations.

Suddenly his address is interrupted. It is a scene second only to that of Pentecost, for the Holy Ghost comes down upon these Gentile converts, and they begin to speak with tongues, to the surprise of St. Peter and his companions. If any lingering feeling of Jewish superiority had been left in their hearts, this unmistakable proof of God's gracious purposes towards the Gentiles destroyed it for ever.

If special grace and special gifts were thus bestowed from Heaven, St. Peter, as head of the Church on earth, must not fear to admit them to every privilege it was his to bestow, and he therefore desired that they should be baptized.

Thus began that mission to the Gentiles which opened a new era in the world's history.

The Apostles had thought much of the blessings and honours intended for their own people, but they had not fully comprehended how broad, how extended Christ's kingdom was to become. So God wonderfully interposed, and called into His service one who was better fitted to be the Apostle of the Gentiles than St. Peter with his zeal, or St. John with his ardent love, —even Paul the persecutor, but afterwards the great and glorious servant of the Christian Church.

CHAPTER II.

The city of Antioch, in Syria, was full of fugitives from other countries.

Many had come from Jerusalem, many also from the adjacent island of Cyprus, others again from Cyrene; and when the truth was preached to them, a great multitude turned to God.

Tidings of this went to Jerusalem, and St. Barnabas was appointed to go to Antioch to instruct the converts more fully in the doctrines they had received, and shortly afterwards, Saul went to assist his labours.

The people of Antioch gave the name of "Christians" to these followers of Christ. Before this the disciples had called themselves "brethren," or "saints," while the Jews in scorn termed them "Nazarenes."

St. Barnabas, with the help of Saul, had been teaching about a year, when some prophets came down from Jerusalem, one of whom, named Agabus, proclaimed a famine throughout Judea.

When the Christians at Antioch heard of the great price of food, and the consequent distress among their brethren in Jerusalem, they collected together a sum of money, and St. Barnabas and Saul conveyed this gift to the sufferers.

But a greater evil than famine troubled the Christian Church—the persecuting cruelty of Herod Agrippa, who had killed James, the brother of John, and now would have taken also the life of St. Peter, had not God interposed, delivering him by the help of an angel.

When St. Barnabas with Saul returned to Antioch, they were accompanied by a young man named John Mark, and probably they would have continued long in their united work, had not the Holy Ghost inspired them to begin that mission to heathen lands to which they were more directly called.

It was about this time that Saul exchanged his name for Paul—a name more pleasing to the ears of Greeks and Romans.

Somewhat near the Feast of Pentecost, in the year 44, the Apostles started from Seleucia, the nearest seaport to Antioch, arriving, after a few hours' sail, at Salamis, a large city on the coast of Cyprus, the birthplace of St. Barnabas.

They began at once to preach in the synagogues, but with no very marked success; however, neither Jews nor idolaters attacked them, or made any opposition to their teaching, until they came to Paphos.

The governor of the island at that time was Sergius Paulus, who, though a Roman and a pagan, was not content with the false deities he had been taught to worship.

At his court there was a false prophet and sorcerer named Bar-Jesus, who had called himself "Elymas," which signifies "the wise one."

When Sergius Paulus heard of the arrival of the Apostles he sent for them to come to him. Perhaps some hope was roused in his heart of hearing from these strangers some truth which would satisfy him.

When St. Barnabas taught of Christ, Elymas the sorcerer began to deny and contradict his words, until the governor said he knew not whom to believe.

St. Paul, appealing to Heaven, called down the punishment of blindness upon this impious man, which so strongly impressed Sergius Paulus with belief in the power of God, that he at once avowed himself a Christian.

"Oh, full of all guile"—thus had the Apostle addressed the sorcerer—"Oh, full of all guile and of all deceit, child of the devil, enemy of all justice, thou ceasest not to pervert the right ways of the Lord. And now, behold, the hand of the Lord is upon thee, and thou shalt be blind, not seeing the sun for a time."

Even as the servant of God spoke, a mist came before the eyes of Elymas, then light faded into a deep, terrible darkness, and blind and helpless he was led to his own home.

Their mission to Cyprus concluded, the Apostles journeyed to Pamphylia, landing at Perga, where there was a celebrated temple dedicated to Diana.

On arriving here, the young companion of Barnabas, "John Mark," determined to return to Jerusalem—probably he shrank from the difficulties and perils which threatened their missionary life.

Together then did Paul and Barnabas proceed on their way, through mountain passes, and across bleak plains, until they reached Antioch in Pisidia—not the city of Antioch in which they had already laboured.

Upon the Jewish Sabbath they directed their steps to the synagogue, where they were invited by the "elders" to address the people.

St. Paul stood up, and in forcible, eloquent words gave a rapid sketch of the history of the Jewish nation, showing that the promises to the line of David were fulfilled in the coming of Christ.

He next proved to them that from this Saviour, this God-man, who had lived and died in their own day, all might receive pardon of sin, and, lastly, he warned his hearers not to incur the dreadful punishment which awaited those who rejected the word of the Almighty.

Some who heard these things were deeply impressed, and followed the Apostles to receive instruction; some had listened with delight to an appeal which showed the preacher's familiar acquaintance with the traditions of their forefathers, but their hearts were not gained for God.

When the next Sabbath came, an immense throng made its way to the synagogue, and this public demonstration of interest roused the anger of the unbelieving Jews, who uttered terrible blasphemies against the name of Jesus, and tried to silence His Apostles.

But neither St. Paul nor Barnabas was afraid. They told these angry Jews that to them had God's grace first been offered, they had been His own chosen and beloved people, but now, as they would not hear, the Divine message was sent to the Gentiles.

Enmity against the Apostles now ran so high that they were forced to leave the city, and on passing out they shook from their feet the dust of Antioch, as

Christ had commanded them to do in such a case.

The Jews perfectly comprehended the meaning of this ceremony. They, when they reached the borders of their own land, were in the habit of carefully wiping from their sandals the smallest particle of dust, so that not so much as a grain of the sacred soil might fall on ground which was unblessed.

When, therefore, they saw Paul and Barnabas pause and shake from their feet the dust of Antioch, they knew that *they* were regarded as heathen and idolaters—no longer the people beloved of God.

Some hundred miles eastward stood Iconium, and there the Apostles made their way, preaching with such power in the synagogue that great numbers both of Jews and Gentiles believed.

But again the hard-hearted multitude made efforts to raise a persecution against these messengers of Christ, although they were not so violent as the Jews of Antioch, so that, in spite of opposition, the Apostles remained some time in Iconium, performing by God's power many miracles there.

These wonderful proofs of Divine greatness caused much excitement, and the enemies of the Christian party became so infuriated that they would have stoned the Apostles to death, unless they had escaped and fled to Lystra.

In that city was a poor cripple who had been lame from his birth. He was known by every one, yet none pitied, none cared for him; and as he heard St. Paul tell of the love and compassion of Jesus, he longed to know more of One Who was so good and kind.

The eye of the Apostle had noted this man who heard him with such rapt attention, and he was inspired by God to heal his infirmity. "Stand upright on thy feet," commanded St. Paul, and immediately the cripple leaped up from the spot where he had been crouching — not standing only, but walking as perfectly as though he had possessed the power from his infancy.

We can partly imagine the excitement such a marvellous event would cause amongst the people, and in their surprise they shouted, "The gods are come down to us in the likeness of men."

Old pagan stories told that the gods sometimes assumed a human form for the purpose of visiting and helping the people of earth, and therefore these idolaters believed St. Barnabas must be their own god Jupiter, while St. Paul, by reason of his wonderful eloquence, could be none other than Mercury.

The report spread rapidly throughout the town, and when it reached the ears of the priest of Jupiter, he hastened to show his reverence to these visitors who were supposed to have descended from heaven. Meantime the Apostles had gone quietly to the dwelling of some Christians, who entertained them during their stay in the city. Presently they were disturbed by the news that two bulls, decorated with garlands, had been brought to the gates as an offering, and that a vast crowd of people had met there for the purpose of worshipping them. The Apostles were very much troubled, and, rending their garments, as was the custom of the Jews in any moment of great grief, they hastened to prevent the people offering the proposed sacrifice, telling them that their only desire in visiting the city was to persuade them to turn from such idolatry, and worship the one true and living God.

But the enemies of the Apostle Paul had pursued him even to Lystra, and these now exercised so strong and so evil an influence over the fickle people, that they were persuaded to stone him whom they had sought to worship.

Thinking him to be dead, they dragged St. Paul's body outside the city gates, exulting over his destruction. But God was protecting His servant, and, with that power which can do all things, He now interposed; for, while the little group of Christians stood mourning and weeping by the side of their teacher, he rose up in their midst, and reviving, went home with them.

Next day both SS. Paul and Barnabas left Lystra, and went to Derbe, a city in which dwelt a man named Gaius, who was rich and highly esteemed.

In the Epistle to the Romans he is mentioned as one who rendered many services to the Church, and it is believed that by his influence the malicious Jews were not allowed to interfere with the teaching of the Apostles, and therefore multitudes were converted.

After remaining there some time, SS. Paul and Barnabas returned to visit those whom they had already converted at Lystra, Iconium, and Antioch, who received them with great joy.

Among the new disciples at Iconium was a young maiden named Thecla, who, during the absence of the Apostles, had been chosen to risk her life for God's truth—the first female martyr. When she was dragged before the pagan judges, she firmly resisted all their attempts to force her to renounce the Christian faith; they threatened, they tortured her, yet she was not afraid. At last Thecla was exposed to the cruelty of the wild beasts in the amphitheatre, but they came crouching to the feet of the virgin Saint, so beloved of God. The crowd who looked on were so moved by this spectacle that they demanded the maiden's release, and the judges dared not resist them; so Thecla ended her days peacefully serving and praising God. Nevertheless, she has received the title of "martyr," and her name placed next to that of St. Stephen, because, in the early ages of the Church, they who had suffered torments for God's sake, which they could not have survived excepting by miraculous help from Heaven, were thus called.

While SS. Paul and Barnabas made this second visit to the cities where already their preaching had brought forth fruit, they formed rules for the orderly government of the Churches. Then, passing again into Pamphylia, through Perga, to Attalia, and thence to Antioch in Syria, they closed their first mission.

CHAPTER III.

For some years the Apostles remained labouring amongst the people of Antioch, but at length a trouble arose, through the disputing of the Christian Jews.

It was very difficult to them to divest themselves of the idea, that in the exact observance of the Mosaic law lay the one way of justification and salvation.

It was very difficult, again, for them to believe that faith and obedience to the law taught by Jesus Christ was sufficient without the outward ceremonies to which they had been accustomed, and which were peculiar to them as a nation. When, therefore, the Christian Jews refused to communicate with the Christian Gentiles until they submitted to the rites of the old Hebrew law, SS. Paul and Barnabas went to Jerusalem, there to confer upon such matters with St. Peter, and SS. James and John.

St. Peter, as head of the Church, addressed the assembly first. He told them that God had given His Holy Spirit to the Gentile as well as to the Jew; nor did He require them to conform to the Jewish customs as regarded meats, and drinks, and outward ceremonies. When he had finished, both St. Paul and St. Barnabas spoke in turn of their mission, and the success granted to their labours.

St. James then addressed the assembly, and said that the Jews could observe the customs in which they had been educated, but that the Gentiles were not to do the same. They must seek to abstain from idolatry.

The final decision of this first council, known as the Council of Jerusalem, was, that the Gentile converts were only obliged to abstain from meats offered in sacrifice, from blood and the flesh of strangled animals, and also were to preserve purity of manners as a distinctive mark of their connection with the Church of Christ.

It was necessary to prohibit these converts from meats offered in sacrifice, else they might easily have fallen back into paganism: impurity was thought so lightly of by the un-christian, that it was necessary to set a higher principle before them as a positive law and obligation. The prohibition against strangulated meats originated in the consideration of what was healthful, while the prohibition from blood had a still higher signification. While it continued to be offered in the temple as a sacrifice to God, it must be reserved wholly for sacred purposes.

The decision of the council was made known to the different Churches, and SS. Paul and Barnabas were sent again to Antioch.

Paul soon began to think of visiting the Churches they had established. "Let us return and visit our brethren in all the cities wherein we have preached the word of the Lord, to see how they do."

St. Barnabas agreed, but he wished to take his nephew John Mark with them, for he also had come to Antioch. St. Paul objected. John Mark had deserted them at Perga through fear of the difficulties which lay before them, and it did not seem expedient to take one who could not endure hardships for the love of Christ.

Then—these two Apostles who had so long been united in God's work could not agree upon this one point, and therefore they parted company, Barnabas sailing for Cyprus, taking John Mark with him, while St. Paul went to the Churches in Asia Minor, having Silas for a helper. We see here that even Christ's own Apostles were not perfectly free from those imperfections and risings of human nature which men are prone to. Doubtless this disagreement was permitted by God for their humiliation, and also for the good of others in the wider diffusion of the Gospel, through the separation of their work.

St. Paul first visited the Churches of Northern Syria, Cilicia, and Lycaonia. At Lystra he was joined by the young Timothy, who had a great desire to help in the missionary work. He was the son of a Greek father and a Jewish mother, and believing that by undergoing the old rite of circumcision he could more easily gain access to the Jews, St. Paul desired him to submit to it.

With Silas in their company, these two messengers of God's truth travelled on until they reached Troas, at which place St. Luke, the physician and evangelist, joined them.

While they remained there a vision was sent to St. Paul in a dream at night. It appeared that a man of Macedonia cried to him, saying, "Pass over into Macedonia and help us."

From this the Apostle believed that God wished him to preach the Gospel there, and therefore he embarked in a ship with his companions, staying, on their first landing, at Philippi, the chief city.

There was no synagogue in this place, for but a very few Jews dwelt there; yet in a little quiet enclosed space by the riverside, the true God was worshipped by a small assembly of Christians, chiefly women. On the Sabbath the Apostles went to preach to them.

One of the women was not of the people of Philippi; she was but staying there while she tried to sell some of the richly-dyed purple or scarlet cloth, which was so greatly prized at that time for its brilliant colour. Her name was Lydia, and she was not a Christian;

but when from the eloquent lips of St. Paul she heard the story of the wonderful life, and still more wonderful death, of Jesus of Nazareth, her heart opened to receive the truth, and she and all her household were converted.

In that city of Philippi there was a female slave, through whom, it was supposed, the pagan gods were accustomed to speak, and therefore she managed to gain money for her owner by appearing to foretell future events.

When this poor creature saw the Apostles going about the streets of Philippi, she used to cry out, "These men are the servants of the Most High God, who preach unto you the way of salvation."

One day as she uttered these words, St. Paul pitied her, and pausing, said to the evil spirit which possessed her,

"I command thee, in the name of Jesus Christ, to go out from her."

That Holy Name had power then as in later days, and in that same hour the evil spirit departed from the poor slave, much to the displeasure of her masters, who could now gain no more money by the strange predictions of future things she had been accustomed to utter.

In their rage they seized St. Paul and Silas and dragged them before the magistrates, complaining that they disturbed the public order by teaching unlawful customs to the people.

The Romans had a law which forbade the teaching of any new religion unless it was one of which the government had already approved. This law St. Paul had certainly broken, that he might obey the higher law of God, but neither he nor his companions had occasioned any disturbance in the city.

The magistrates made no attempt to discover the truth of the complaint made to them, and seeing that the people were angrily resolved on having the offenders punished, they ordered St. Paul and Silas to be beaten.

The Jews, in scourging, were not permitted to inflict more than thirty-nine blows, but the Romans used rods of elm, and gave many more stripes, so that Paul and Silas were all bruised and bleeding from the treatment they had received, when they were led away to prison.

The gaoler had orders to keep them securely, and they were thrust into the close inner prison with their feet fastened in stocks, so that they were prevented from taking any rest.

During the night, the prisoners who were confined in another part of the prison heard voices singing—singing God's praises from the miserable dungeon. Suddenly, while the Apostles sang, an earthquake shook the prison to its very foundations, every door burst open, and the bands of every captive were loosed.

The keeper of the prison awoke from sleep, and when he saw what had happened, and that the doors were open, he trembled with fear, for he naturally believed that all the prisoners would have escaped, and knew that his own life would be the forfeit.

Drawing his sword, he was about to kill himself. Death was inevitable, so by his own hand he would die; but in this moment of despair, the voice of St. Paul reached him. "Do thyself no harm," said the Apostle, "for we are all here."

Calling for a light, the gaoler entered the dungeon. Yes, there indeed were his prisoners; and falling down trembling and tearful at their feet, he said, "Masters, what must I do to be saved?" It was given him in that moment to know that the scourged, imprisoned men before him were the servants and messengers of Almighty God.

"Believe in the Lord Jesus, and thou shalt be saved and thy house." That was what they had to tell him; and the gaoler took them out of the dungeon and washed their wounds, and bringing them to his own house, set food before them, and begged for instruction in the Christian faith. Then, with all his family, this man received the grace of

Baptism; and when morning came, a message was brought from the magistrates bidding the gaoler release his prisoners.

But St. Paul said that they would not thus depart. They had been scourged, they had been thrust into the dungeon without an opportunity of proving their innocence, and he then declared himself a citizen of Rome, requiring the magistrates to make known that they had been wrongfully punished.

The authorities of the city were afraid when the Apostle's words were repeated to them. To scourge a Roman citizen publicly and uncondemned was a serious offence against Roman law. So, coming to St. Paul and Silas, they acknowledged they had acted unlawfully and entreated them to depart, which the Apostles did after bidding farewell to their Christian friends in the house of Lydia.

St. Luke, with Timothy, who had not been taken before the magistrates, remained in the city to instruct the Philippian Church more fully.

Travelling onwards many miles, Paul and Silas reached Thessalonica, the city next in importance to Philippi, wherein many Jews were living. At first they were disposed to listen to the teaching of the Apostles, but hearing that the Gentiles were to be equally partakers with themselves in the privileges and graces offered, they began to murmur loudly and excite the anger of the people, who cried out that the strange men were proclaiming another to be king—Jesus the Nazarene—in the place of the great Cæsar!

The mob went to the house of Jason, where the Apostles were lodging, intending to seize them, but, as they were absent, Jason himself was seized and brought before the magistrates, upon a charge of having such persons at his house.

The magistrates made the Christians of the city and Jason also promise that no further excitement and disturbance should occur, so in the darkness and silence of night St. Paul and Silas had to escape from Thessalonica.

They were not discouraged or daunted by this opposition to the truths they preached, they sought only to obey the command of their Master, Who had bidden them carry His Gospel to every creature.

Another fifty miles of journeying, and they were at Berea. Here they found more sympathy than they had met with in Thessalonica, but their persecutors followed them into Berea, seeking to rouse the malice of the unbelieving against the Apostles, so that those who were Christians and loved St. Paul entreated him to escape, and even went with him down to the sea-shore and saw him safely embarked in a ship sailing for Athens.

Silas and Timothy had remained in Berea to instruct and confirm the faithful there, so the Apostle Paul was alone in the beautiful city of Athens, surrounded by glorious temples and costly statues, and all the marks of civilisation of which it was the centre. As he observed the gorgeous temples raised in honour of every known pagan god, St. Paul felt a burning desire to preach to the Athenians of the great

Father in heaven, and Jesus Christ, His eternal Son.

Going to the Jewish synagogue, he addressed the Jews assembled there, and then went to the large square, called the Agora, in which the market was held.

Here many people were in the habit of meeting to hear and to tell news, and the Apostle had *his* great, glorious news to utter—the tidings of a Saviour born into the world, dying for the world, risen from the grave, and ascended to the right hand of God, the Father Almighty—which were unknown themes to the men of Athens.

A flight of sixteen steps led from this Agora to Mars Hill, upon which was built a temple in honour of Mars, god of war.

Here, too, was the great court of

justice, called the Areopagus, and the judges were the most learned men of Athens, who tried all matters of government, and pronounced sentence upon criminals. The Stoics and Epicureans led St. Paul here—to the supreme tribunal—that he might speak about his God.

CHAPTER IV.

In the Acts of the Apostles we have the address which St. Paul delivered with eloquent tongue and flashing eye to the astonished audience.

He told them that in their capital he had seen one nameless altar—an altar "to the unknown God"—an altar which they had erected, lest there might, in some other land, be a God of whom they knew not.

"What, therefore, you worship without knowing it, that I preach to you. God, Who made the world, and all things therein, He, being Lord of heaven and earth, dwelleth not in temples made with hands."

Thus did he commence his instruction, to which the men of Athens at first listened with interest and attention, but when he came to dwell upon the doctrine of the resurrection of the dead they laughed him to scorn.

A few, however, believed that St. Paul spoke truly, and these sought further instruction from him during his stay in Athens. Among their number was a humble woman named Damaris, and Dionysius, one of the members of the Areopagus. For a short time Timothy came to assist the Apostle in his work at Athens, but he was wanted in Thessalonica, and therefore speedily returned there, while St. Paul went on alone to the city of Corinth, where he had neither companion nor friend.

The Emperor Claudius had issued

a proclamation, commanding the Jews to leave Rome, and one of these named Aquila, with Priscilla his wife, had taken up his abode in Corinth. With them St. Paul obtained a lodging, partly because Aquila was a tent-maker, and the Apostle in his younger days had learned that trade.

Now that food was scarce throughout Greece, and he had none to assist him, St. Paul had to employ himself and work hard during the week, but always when the Sabbath came round, and the Jews assembled in the synagogue, he was there to tell the Corinthians the new law of Christ Jesus.

A great number of Jewish people were opposed to such strange doctrines, but the Apostle met with greater success amongst the Greeks, and soon formed a little congregation of Christians.

After labouring about three months alone, St. Paul was encouraged by the arrival of Silas and Timothy. There was much to tell about their work, and Timothy spoke of the faith and of the love of the Christians in Thessalonica, but they had fallen into some errors, which St. Paul reproved in his letter of holy counsel, known to us as the First Epistle to the Thessalonians.

Silas and Timothy had brought a gift of money to the Apostle from the Churches of Macedonia, so that he was not forced to spend so many hours at his trade, and had therefore more time for instructing and preaching. Among those people of Corinth who had been received into the Christian Church was Crispus, the chief ruler of the synagogue—and his entire household had also opened their minds to truth.

This made the Jews extremely angry, and they spoke so blasphemously of Christ that St Paul could not bear to hear them. Shaking his garment with a gesture of horror and indignation, he cried, "Your blood be upon your own head; I am clean: from henceforth I will go unto the Gentiles." And so saying he left the synagogue and went to the dwelling of Justus, who, being a pious man, allowed the Apostle to teach there.

In a vision of the night God encouraged His servant, saying to him, "Do not fear, but speak, and hold not thy peace. Because I am with thee, and no man shall set on thee to hurt thee, for I have much people in this city."

After this declaration of God's Will St. Paul remained in Corinth for another year and half.

He had already, as we have seen, written one epistle to the Thessalonians, and a few months later he wrote them a second. Some of the people of Thessalonica had fallen into a mistake.

Thinking that Christ was soon coming to judge the world, they deemed it useless to occupy themselves in their different callings.

When they left off work, like all other idle, unemployed people, they began to meddle with the concerns of their neighbours, and in his second letter St. Paul warned them that a great many things were to happen before the second coming of Christ, and he told them also the rule, "If any man will not work neither let him eat." He begged them to pray that the Word of God might bring forth much fruit among the Corinthian people, and bid them hold firmly to the traditions received from him.

After a time a new governor named Gallio came to Corinth, and the unbelieving Jews took this opportunity of trying to injure the Apostle. Taking him before a magistrate, they accused him of teaching men to worship God after a manner contrary to law. Before the Apostle could attempt to defend this charge, Gallio said he would not listen to such a complaint, and he sent the angry people away.

The Greeks were very much vexed at this attempt of the Jews to bring trouble upon St. Paul, and they seized Sosthenes, the chief ruler of the synagogue, and beat him before the judgment-seat, and yet even then Gallio did not interfere.

It seems probable that the Apostle would seek out Sosthenes after this rough treatment, and gain his friendship; at any rate, we next hear of this Jewish ruler as a Christian, and also a companion of St. Paul in his journey to Ephesus.

About a month following the day upon which he had been taken before Gallio, the Apostle left Corinth with Aquila and Priscilla, whom he left at Ephesus, while he himself passed on to Jerusalem to keep the Feast of Pentecost.

In the city of Ephesus stood the widely celebrated temple of Diana, which was one of the seven wonders of the world. It had taken more than two hundred years to build, and it was made of the purest marble. It had one hundred and twenty pillars, thirty-six of which were most beautifully carved, and the others polished; every one had been the gift of some king.

The temple was not roofed over, excepting just in the part where the image of Diana stood — the ugly log of wood, with a head adorned with a mural crown, and the body covered with figures of animals.

The superstitious people believed that this idol had fallen from the sky, and during our month of May they held a great feast in Diana's honour, to which people came from far and near in vast crowds.

In this city they also practised magic. Certain words were written on parchment, which had been copied from the image of the goddess, and this parchment was worn upon the body to charm away evil spirits, and to heal diseases, as it was believed.

We cannot marvel that ignorant people were thus led astray, when the wise and learned philosophers of Greece had begun to write about these hidden things, and sell such books at enormous prices.

It was to Ephesus, the city filled with pagan superstition and practice, that St. Paul came after his visit to Jerusalem, meeting there again the Christians Aquila and Priscilla.

During the absence of the Apostle a young man had been preaching in the synagogue, who was a Jew of the name of Apollos.

He was well versed in Mosaic law and the books of the Old Testament, but he could teach nothing of Christ, for he did not believe that the promised Messiah had indeed come into the world.

It was from Aquila and Priscilla that Apollos learned the Christian faith, and then in his gratitude and love he longed to make it known to others, and for this purpose went to Corinth, where he induced many Jews to listen and to believe.

When St. Paul came back to stay a while in Ephesus he resumed his trade, and taught continually in the synagogue; but at length the ill-feeling of the Jews broke out upon him, and they spoke evilly of him, and blasphemed the Name of Jesus.

Upon this the Apostle left the synagogue and hired a room, where he taught the Word of God, and many were converted and baptized, and received the Holy Ghost from the hands of the Apostle.

It pleased the Almighty to work

miraculous cures by means of St. Paul, as we read: "God wrought by the hand of Paul more than common miracles. So that even there were brought from his body to the sick, handkerchiefs and aprons, and the diseases departed from them, and the wicked spirits went out of them."

Then some of the people who had witnessed the wonders which St. Paul could do in the name of Jesus, thought they also could do the same. There was a Jew who had seven sons, and these men wanted to drive out an evil spirit with which a person was possessed. But when they bade it come from him, the devil spoke from within the man, and said, "Jesus I know, and Paul I know, but who are you?" and the possessed leaped upon and overcame them, so that they had to escape.

When this was told in Ephesus, the people were awed, for they could not but see that God would not permit His Name to be taken in vain, and they began to be so much afraid of practising their magic arts that they brought out the wicked books, which treated of hidden things, and publicly burned them.

During St. Paul's stay at Ephesus he went over for a short time to visit the Christians in Corinth, and to his great sorrow he found that among them were some who had brought disgrace upon their faith by relapsing into many of their heathenish customs.

After he had again returned to Ephesus, such bad news came about the Corinthian Church that St. Paul wrote them a letter, in which he reproved their sins and entreated them to lead holy lives. This letter is the First Epistle to the Corinthians.

About this time a disturbance arose in Ephesus because the men who had formerly sold models of the pagan goddess Diana could not now find an easy sale for these things, and were therefore enraged with St. Paul for preaching against idolatry.

A silversmith of the city, whose name was Demetrius, called together all who followed his own trade, and represented to them how much they had lost through this man who preached the new faith and persuaded the people to renounce the gods they had formerly worshipped.

Ephesus was soon in a tumult, and the angry people resolved to seize upon St. Paul, whom they considered had done them great injury; but on going to find him in the house of Aquila, he was not there. Instead of the Apostle, therefore, two other Christians were captured and brought to the place where all public meetings were held.

St. Paul was not long in receiving tidings of this occurrence, and he would have hastened to the assembled crowd had not his friends interfered, for they believed that in their rage the excited people might do him some serious injury.

"Great is Diana of the Ephesians!" —so rose the cry again and again, and it was a difficult matter for the authorities to quiet them.

In this occurrence the Apostle saw an indication of God's Will that he should depart from Ephesus,—at any rate, for a time,—therefore he called together the Christians, and after exhorting them to perseverance in the faith they had embraced, and to a holy and blameless life, he bade them farewell.

For three years he had taught in that city, but now, with Timothy for a helper, he was to teach in other places, and win more hearts to a knowledge and love of the true God.

He now made his way to Troas, where once before he had stayed, though only for a short time. But St. Paul's heart was troubled regarding the Corinthian Church: Titus had been sent there, but he had not returned, and St. Paul resolved to go and meet him.

Leaving Troas he went to Philippi, where he was welcomed with great joy by his friends, and after a time Titus found him bringing better news of the people of Corinth, the greater number of whom were striving to obey the counsels contained in his letter. There were, however, some who still refused to submit to the Apostle's authority, and who were wicked enough to utter untruthful things of him. They said that the money he wished the Christian Churches to collect for their poorer friends, was really needed by himself. It was now that St. Paul wrote his Second Epistle to the Corinthians, in which he encouraged those who were trying to live a holy life, and this letter he sent by the hand of Titus, while he himself visited Thessalonica and Berea.

After summer and autumn had passed, the Apostle went to Corinth, but scarcely had he arrived than he heard of troubles in the Church of Galatia, because some people of Jerusalem had been there, endeavouring to sow disbelief and distrust in the teaching of St. Paul.

A letter was therefore written by him to the Galatians, to warn them against these false doctors who were preaching the obligation of observing the Mosaic law.

Now the Apostle began to attend to the Church in Corinth, reproving error and sin, and separating those who would not obey the law of Christ from the submissive and good. He had warned them many times before he did this, but now he could not permit to be numbered among the followers of Christ those who brought shame upon their profession by openly disobeying His laws.

There were connected with the Christian Churches pious women, who were called "deaconesses." Their charge was to assist the sick, to instruct the catechumens, and help the newly baptized to lead a Christian life. For these duties it was necessary to have persons of experience and great piety, and therefore the age for their admission to the office was first fixed at sixty, but afterwards at forty years.

One of these deaconesses, named Phœbe, was about leaving Corinth for Rome, and by her St. Paul sent an epistle to the people of that city.

He had not yet been there, but he hoped before long to visit the Church which was then being formed, and meanwhile he sent them this proof of love and good-will. It was written in Greek, but for the benefit of those who did not understand that language was translated into Latin. In the arrangement of the Scriptures, this Epistle is always placed first—although not the first which the Apostle's hand has written—because of the great importance of its contents, as well as the pre-eminence of the place to which it was sent.

In it the Apostle first commends the faith of the Romans whom he long to see, "that I may impart unto you some spiritual grace to strengthen you." He goes on to show how the shameful sins of the pagans were the result of the lack of faith and of humility.

He next censures those Jews who, while they boast of the law, neglect to keep it, and while admitting the advantages of the Jew, "because the words of God were committed to them," he teaches that all men, whether Jew or Gentile, are sinners who must be saved by the grace of God, and not alone by obedience to the law.

This doctrine of salvation by Christ

is dwelt upon continually, but St. Paul also insists upon the necessity of good works, and that a Christian must die to sin and self, and live unto God.

He also gives many beautiful counsels regarding Christian virtues, lessons of obedience to superiors and of mutual charity. He bids the strong bear with the weak, and cautions Christians not to judge and condemn each other, neither to give scandal.

Then, exhorting them all to be "of one mind one towards another according to Jesus Christ," he promises to come and visit them, and concludes by invoking upon them the grace of God " to Whom be honour and glory for ever and ever."

CHAPTER V.

The time was approaching when St. Paul was to leave Corinth—not sailing thence to Jerusalem as he had planned, but returning by the way he had come, because he found that some of the unbelieving Jews had formed a scheme to destroy him while upon his journey.

For the space of a week the Apostle remained at Troas, and upon the last evening he had assembled the Christians together in an upper room—one of those dining-halls which the Latins termed *cænacula*.

The Scripture narrative tells us that they were there to " break bread," the name usually given in those days to the celebration of the Holy Mysteries. The Body and Blood of our Lord was received by those early Christians with extreme care and the profoundest reverence, but in that age the Church had not ordained that the reception of the Eucharist should take place in the morning and fasting. This rule prevailed at the close of the first century out of respect to so great a mystery. In the time of the Apostles the Communion was given at other parts of the day, and thus we understand the passage referring to this meeting of Christians upon the last evening of St. Paul's stay in Corinth.

An unusual crowd appears to have been assembled, and the heat was so great that the windows were left open. A young man named Eutychus, sitting in the recess of one of these windows, being overcome with sleep, fell through it to the ground. St. Paul at once descended, to find Eutychus, as it seemed, lifeless, but stretching himself upon the body, he besought God to manifest His power, and then returned to the upper room, and continued teaching till the day dawned.

Eutychus soon joined the assembly, perfectly restored by the power of the Almighty through His servant.

St. Luke, with Timothy and others who proposed accompanying the great Apostle on his journey, went down to the ship, but St. Paul had decided to travel on foot to the place at which it would next stop, called Assos, where he entered the vessel and went on to Miletus, situated some thirty-five miles from Ephesus.

At Miletus he sent a message asking

some of the bishops and priests to come down to the ship and pray with him. They talked together upon the shore, and St. Paul told them that he was bound for Jerusalem. "I go to Jerusalem not knowing the things which shall befall me there. Save, that the Holy Ghost in every city witnesseth to me, saying that bands and afflictions await me at Jerusalem." He conjured the bishops to guard the people confided to their care, and warned them against false teachers, who would seek to mislead them, and then he bade them farewell. We read that there was weeping among them all, for they feared from his words that they should see the face of their teacher and father no more; and as the vessel sailed from Miletus they returned to Ephesus with heavy hearts.

At Tyre the ship had to unload, and St. Paul with his companions availed themselves of this opportunity of going on shore to find out the Christians who dwelt in that part. Seven days they remained amongst the disciples they found there; and one who had the power of understanding some of the things which were to happen, warned the Apostle of the great danger which threatened him at Jerusalem.

But St. Paul knew that his way was ordered by God Who could shield him from every danger if such was His Divine Will, therefore he would not be persuaded to alter his course.

The Christians of Tyre went with him to the shore and knelt down while he blessed them, and so they parted, and the ship sailed on to Ptolemais.

There the Apostles left the vessel

and pursued their way by land, staying at Cæsarea in the house of Philip the Evangelist, whose four daughters had the gift of prophecy. During St. Paul's visit, there came down from Judea a prophet, named Agabus, who took the girdle of the Apostle, and binding his own hands and feet with it, said, "Thus saith the Holy Ghost. The man whose girdle this is, the Jews shall bind in this manner in Jerusalem, and shall deliver into the hands of the Gentiles."

St. Luke and Timothy then entreated their companion not to go to Jerusalem, but he would not listen to them.

"What do you mean, weeping and afflicting my heart?" he said, "For I am ready not only to be bound, but to die also in Jerusalem for the Name of the Lord Jesus."

When the Apostle uttered these words, the others besought him no longer, but said, " The Will of the Lord be done," and thus—the one with heart filled with courage and even with desire to die for Christ, the others with sorrow mingled with their confidence in God—they went on to Jerusalem.

Arriving in that city, St. Paul was received with the greatest joy by all the Christians, and next day the Apostle James, the Bishop of Jerusalem, convened a meeting of all who composed the Church.

To them St. Paul gave a report of his work during his four years' absence. When he had concluded his address, he was told that great numbers of the Jews in that city believed the Gospel, yet were very strict in their observance of Mosaic law, and that they were hostile because they believed St. Paul taught the Jews of other places to neglect the customs of their people.

St. James advised that, to prove this belief unfounded, the Apostle should go to the temple upon the next day, which was the feast of Pentecost, and take part in a certain ceremony for four of the faithful.

These four men had taken a vow. The Jews frequently did this for some special purpose, either that they might be delivered from some danger, or to show their gratitude for some special blessing. Vows were made for a certain time, during which the person considered himself specially consecrated to Almighty God, and he had to observe strict rules, such as to abstain from drinking wine, or from shaving his head. When the time had come to an end, it was the duty of the person who had made the vow to appear in the temple, taking his offerings. Offerings on such an occasion were costly, and it was a customary thing for some richer and pious Jew to pay this amount for the man whose vow was at an end.

It was for this purpose that St. James proposed St. Paul accompanying to the temple the four men who now accomplished the vow of the Nazarite, so that the Jews might observe his respect for their ancient law.

Scarcely had the Apostle shown himself than some Jews, who had come up from Asia for the festival, saw him, and pointed him out to their fanatical companions as one who despised the law and profaned the temple.

A terrible uproar followed, and seizing the Apostle, they cried, " Men of

Israel, help: this is the man that teacheth all men everywhere against the people, and the law, and this place, and moreover hath brought in Gentiles into the temple, violating this holy place."

St. Paul was thus dragged from the temple to the outer court, and the gates were closed, while the angry people began beating their prisoner, and would certainly have killed him had not word been taken to the Roman tribune Lysias, who sent soldiers and centurions down to the scene of contest.

Lysias readily believed that the Apostle had committed some serious offence, nevertheless, however guilty, it was not lawful for the mob to punish him, so the soldiers were ordered to bring him in chains to receive judgment. When the captain enquired what was the charge against the prisoner, there was such a confusion that he could not discover the truth, and therefore bade the soldiers lead St. Paul to the castle, the angry crowd following, with cries of "Away with him. Away with him."

When the Apostle was brought into the castle, he turned to Lysias, and asked if he might speak with him, who replied, "Canst thou speak Greek?" Upon hearing that St. Paul was a Jew of Tarsus, he acceded to his request that he might address the people.

"Men, brethren, and fathers," began St. Paul, using the Hebrew language, which was spoken in Jerusalem, and in a moment the tumult was hushed and every ear strained to listen.

The Apostle gave them a sketch of his early history, telling them how *he* once hated and persecuted the Christians, and then of his wondrous journey to Damascus—of his blindness, and its cure.

He passed on to his first visit to Jerusalem, spoke of his vision in the temple, when the Lord Jesus appeared to him, and bade him depart and preach to the Gentiles.

The crowd had heard him thus far with silent attention, but now their rage burst forth afresh.

Were they, the sons of Abraham, to be left for the despised Gentiles? They would not suffer such words to be spoken, and once more they cry, " Away with him." Away with such an one from the earth, for it is not fit that he should live.

They began casting off their heavy outer garments purposing to stone him, but Lysias ordered his soldiers to bring the prisoner within the castle.

He had not understood St. Paul's address, being delivered in Hebrew, but he saw how greatly the people were infuriated, and therefore judged that some terrible crime must have been committed.

He accordingly told one of the centurions to scourge the prisoner, so that he might confess what he had done, and St. Paul was bound to a low pillar that he might receive this humiliating punishment. But he spoke to the centurion and said, "Is it lawful for you to scourge a man who is a Roman and uncondemned?"

The centurion knew that such a thing was unlawful, so he went to Lysias to tell him that their prisoner was a Roman.

When Lysias found from St. Paul that he was a free-born citizen of Rome, he gave orders for him to be unbound, and convened a meeting of the Jewish council for the next day, before which the Apostle should answer the charges made against him.

Early in the morning this council assembled, just as once it had assembled to judge St. Stephen when Saul, the well-known Pharisee, was one of its members. Now he was a prisoner—Paul, the servant of Jesus Christ, standing before many who knew him as the persecutor of Christians.

"Men and brethren," he said, "I have conversed with all good conscience before God until this present day."

At this the high priest Ananias, in his anger, told those who stood near to strike the prisoner upon the mouth.

Then St. Paul said to him, "God shall strike thee, thou whited wall. For sittest thou to judge me according to the law, and contrary to the law commandest me to be struck?"

The bystanders now accused the Apostle of speaking against the high priest. Seeing that he was not to be fairly tried, St. Paul appealed to the Pharisees who were present. "Men, brethren, I am a Pharisee, the son of a Pharisee. Concerning the hope and resurrection of the dead I am called in question."

At these words a great dissension arose between his judges. Party spirit was kindled immediately in the Pharisees, who, forgetting their anger against the Apostle, now declared that they ound no evil in him. The confusion increased, so that Lysias heard of it, and ordered his soldiers to go and bring back the prisoner to the castle.

It was well that he did so, or St. Paul would have been almost torn to pieces by the indignant Sadducees.

Night drew on, and in the still darkness the Lord Jesus Christ appeared to His servant, speaking softly and encouragingly in his ear: "Be constant; for as thou hast testified of me at Jerusalem, so must thou bear witness also at Rome."

Not to die then! not yet to lay down life for God's truth. To suffer again and to suffer more—yet St. Paul was not dismayed. Had he not said already to the Christians of Ephesus, when upon the sea-shore of Miletus they looked on his face for the last time, "I fear none of these things, neither do I count my life more precious than myself, so that I may consummate my course."

CHAPTER VI.

During that night the enemies of God's servant were not forgetful of him, and forty men bound themselves under a curse neither to eat nor drink until they had succeeded in killing him.

They accordingly made request to the council that Lysias might have St. Paul tried once more, purposing in their hearts to lie in wait as he came out from the castle, and falling upon him, destroy him.

In some manner which we do not know, the secret transpired, and a young man related to the Apostle brought news to the castle of what the forty Zelotes had arranged.

Lysias listened to his story, but bade him not to speak of the discovered plot to any one. He then determined to send St. Paul away that same night, as it was evident that his life was in peril through the malice of the people. Summoning two of his centurions, he bade them make ready two hundred soldiers, seventy horsemen, and two hundred spearmen, who were to take a journey into Cæsarea at nine o'clock that night, and horses were also to be provided for the Apostle, who must be safely placed under the care of Felix the governor of that place.

Lysias knew that this enormous guard would be necessary to ensure the safety of his prisoner. When all was in readiness for departure, he had a letter written which was to be given to the governor of Cæsarea, explaining the reasons for which St. Paul was sent to him, and all who had any accusation to make against him were told to go to Felix with the complaint.

By the dawn of morning, the travellers had accomplished about thirty-five miles of their journey, reaching Antipatris, where the foot-soldiers were dismissed; the rest of the guard conducted the Apostle safely through another day's travel, and then they entered Cæsarea.

After reading the letter sent by Lysias, Felix asked his prisoner from what province he came. St. Paul told him that he was from Cilicia, where he was born.

Felix then gave orders that he should be kept in the judgment-hall of Herod until his accusers came forward, and his defence could be heard.

For several days the Apostle remained thus, until the high priest Ananias, and others of the Jewish council, arrived with a Roman advocate, or lawyer, ready to assist them in making their complaint against him to the Cæsarean governor.

Felix had once been a slave, who by the favour of the Roman emperor had been raised to his high position; but he was an unjust and a tyrannical man, who lived in great sin.

It was before him then that St. Paul had to appear, and Tertullus, the lawyer, commenced his speech by praising Felix, as if he had been a good man, and laying his accusations against the prisoner. First, he was charged with being a "pestilent man, raising seditions among all the Jews throughout the world, and author of the sedition of the sect of the Nazarenes." On these grounds St. Paul was deemed an offender against the Roman government, and against the law of Moses.

The next charge was that he had brought Gentiles into the temple.

The assembled Jews confirmed the truth of what Tertullus uttered, and then Felix gave the prisoner permission to defend himself.

He therefore declared that he was not guilty of disputing with any man, nor had he caused disturbance either in the temple or synagogue; that he had gone up to the temple to engage in a Jewish ceremony, and those who had been in his company were not Gentiles.

After such a defence, it would have seemed impossible to find any plea for detaining the Apostle a prisoner, but

Felix only put the matter off, promising to enquire further into it at the coming of Lysias. Hoping that the Apostle would purchase his freedom, Felix remanded him to a somewhat light imprisonment, which continued two years.

One day the governor sent for St. Paul, that he and his wicked wife Drusilla might hear so famous a teacher speak about his faith.

The Apostle had the gift of making his addresses exactly applicable to those who listened to him; and as he knew the sinful life of Felix, he was not afraid to speak out openly of that purity of life which the Gospel law enjoins.

He spoke also of the judgment to come, in such forcible words that the governor's conscience was awakened, and he trembled.

Still,—like so many wicked people of later times,—he was not ready to give up his sinful pleasures, but only wished to be rid of the thought of God's future punishment. "For this time go thy way;" he said, "when I have a convenient time I will send for thee."

Thus did Felix close his heart to the influence of the Holy Spirit, and resist God's grace; nor do we read that he ever had another opportunity for repentance.

At the close of the two years during which St. Paul was a prisoner, another governor was appointed in place of Felix, whose name was Festus.

Scarcely had he come to Cæsarea than he went to visit Jerusalem, and the Jews took the occasion as a favourable time to ask that Paul might be tried there, but this request was not granted.

When Festus returned to Cæsarea, he had the Apostle brought up before him in the presence of the accusers, and St. Paul replied to the charges against him in much the same words he had used two years before.

Festus was perplexed, for it was evident to him that the prisoner had not created any disturbance against the government; still he feared the Jews, and therefore asked St. Paul if he would not like to go up to Jerusalem for trial. But the Apostle replied that he stood before Cæsar's judgment-seat, and he appealed to Cæsar.

Then Festus cried, "Hast thou appealed to Cæsar? To Cæsar shalt thou go;" meaning that he should be sent to Rome for trial.

Soon after these proceedings, the young King Agrippa, with his sister Bernice, came upon a visit to the governor of Cæsarea, and hearing of St. Paul's case, said that he would himself pronounce judgment upon it.

The great hall of audience was filled with the royal court, the tribunes and all the chief men were assembled; and St. Paul took this opportunity to preach the Gospel to them.

He told the story of his life, of his conversion and subsequent work amongst men; but when he said that Christ had come to be a light to the Gentiles as well as to the Jews, a loud cry broke from Festus, "Paul, thou art beside thyself, much learning hath made thee mad."

"I am not mad, most excellent Festus, but I speak words of truth and soberness," replied the Apostle; then, appealing to the king, he added, "Believest thou the prophets, O King Agrippa? I know that thou believest."

Agrippa said, "Almost thou persuadest me to be a Christian."

"Would to God," cried St. Paul, "that not only thou, but all that hear me this day, should become such as I am, except these bonds."

The king, with Festus and the rest, rose up to leave the hall. "This man hath done nothing that merits either death or the prison," said Agrippa. "He might have been set at liberty if he had not appealed unto Cæsar."

As it was now necessary to send the Apostle to Rome, Festus had him placed with some other prisoners on board a ship which was going part of the way. It was in the year 62 that St.

Paul started as a prisoner, with Luke and Aristarchus to bear him company.

Sidon was the first stopping-place, and here the Apostle was allowed to go on shore to visit the Christians who dwelt there.

When they arrived at Lystra, Julius the centurion, who had charge of the prisoners, found a large ship going to Italy from Alexandria, into which he had them removed. But a contrary wind rose, so that for several days they could proceed but very slowly. It was a time of year when sailing was difficult and dangerous, so when they reached a place called Good Havens, St. Paul said it would be better to remain there during the winter.

But the master of the ship and the centurion determined to go on, hoping to reach Phenice, and winter there.

At first a gentle south wind was blowing, but a sudden change came, and the ship was driven furiously along towards the dangerous coast of Africa. The sailors were afraid that their vessel would be broken to pieces in the storm, and they passed strong chains underneath it and took down all their sails. The next day they tried to make the ship lighter by throwing over all they could most easily spare, and upon the third day they even cast away ropes, sails, and anchors.

It was so dark from the heavy stormy clouds, that the master of the ship could not discover whereabouts they were, and all hope seemed gone.

Then St. Paul stood up in the midst of the frightened men, and bade them take heart, for the life of every one should be preserved, although the vessel would be lost. He gave them his authority for such a promise—"For an Angel of God, Whose I am, and Whom I serve, stood by me this night, saying, Fear not, Paul; thou must be brought before Cæsar; and, behold, God hath given thee all them that sail with thee."

For fourteen long days and nights the vessel was driven about in the sea of Adria, and then the sailors thought they were drawing near land, but upon letting down their measuring line they found the water becoming so shallow that they feared being cast upon the rocks, so they cast down four anchors to hold the ship securely until morning.

Filled, however, with selfish fear, the sailors secretly let down a boat into the water, meaning to get into it themselves, and leave the others in their difficulty. St. Paul was given the power of divining what passed in their hearts, and he told their scheme to the centurion, who ordered his soldiers to cut the ropes that the boat might fall over into the sea.

When day broke, the Apostle begged all on board to eat, and he repeated his promise of safety for all, and taking bread, he "gave thanks to God in the sight of them all," and they also eat and were refreshed.

It was now evident that the ship could not be saved, so the wheat with which it was laden was thrown over, in order that it might be lightened, and so run close in to the shore. But as the sailors were endeavouring to get up a little creek, the vessel stuck fast in the ground, and the hinder part was broken to pieces by the stormy waves.

The soldiers would have begun putting the prisoners to death, lest they might swim to shore and thus escape, but the centurion prevented them, and ordered those who were able to swim to do so, while the rest he made hold on to the boards and broken spars of the ship. In this way every soul was saved of the two hundred and seventy-six who had been on board the vessel—saved for the sake of Paul, the beloved servant and Apostle of God.

The island on which they were cast was called Melita — the Malta of our own day—and no sooner were they landed than a fresh proof of God's providential care over St. Paul was granted.

A fire of sticks had been kindled by the people of the island, and as the Apostle assisted the others, gathering together what faggots he could find, a viper came and fastened upon his hand.

The ignorant natives observing this, thought it must be some very wicked man pursued by dreadful judgments, although he had escaped the perils of the sea; but when St. Paul shook off the viper, and it was seen that he was wholly uninjured by its poisonous bite, they changed in their feelings, and believed he could be nothing less than a god.

It was the Will of Almighty God that still more wonders should be wrought upon that island.

The father of Publius, the governor of Malta, was lying dangerously ill, and St. Paul went to visit him as his Master when on earth visited the sick and suffering, and "laid his hands on him," and healed him.

Seeing this marvel wrought by the touch of the Apostle, all the people of the island who were in any way sick or diseased came hastening to St. Paul, and they too received the healing of their infirmities. For three months the shipwrecked company remained in Malta, and when at length they departed in a ship bound for Italy, the people of the island gave them many presents in gratitude and good-will.

CHAPTER VII.

On arriving at Puteoli (Pozzuoli) St. Paul received a welcome from the Church already formed there, and at last, in the year 63, the eighth of the reign of Nero, he entered the city of Rome, surrounded by the Christians who had gone out to meet him in his chains.

Julius the centurion now gave up his charge to the captain of the emperor's guard, whom we hear of as a just and kind man, who treated St. Paul well, and even permitted him to see his friends, and to teach the Christian faith to such as willed.

For two years this imprisonment

lasted, during which time, Scripture tells us, he "received all that came in to him, preaching the kingdom of God, and teaching the things which concern the Lord Jesus Christ, with all confidence, without prohibition."

Here ceases the narrative of the first missions to the pagan world, given by St. Luke in the Acts of the Apostles. Those first triumphs of the faith were won much as the triumphs of later days —always against unbelief, error, opposition, and calumny; yet won even by an Apostle in chains, as truth must ever conquer, even when apparently vanquished.

That two years' captivity in the Roman capital was cheered by the company of St. Luke, Timothy, and John Mark, who was now a faithful servant of Christ; they could go where St. Paul was not permitted, and take counsels and messages of encouragement from him to the different Churches.

There was a slave named Onesimus, who was very useful to St. Paul, and who became a Christian through his teaching. He had robbed his master and escaped to Rome, where from curiosity he went to hear the imprisoned Apostle tell of Jesus of Nazareth. His heart was touched, and seeking an opportunity, he opened his conscience to St. Paul, in obedience to whom he went back to his master, bearing a letter written to him by the Apostle. This letter is known to us as the Epistle to Philemon. Tychicus accompanied Onesimus on his way, bearing an epistle to the Church of Colosse, which was the city in which Philemon dwelt.

In this beautiful letter St. Paul

exhorts his brethren to beware of the philosophers and Jewish teachers, who would withdraw them from Christ. He entreats them to look after heavenly things and to grow in holiness. He also speaks of the duties of husbands and wives, parents and children, advises constant prayer, and concludes with various salutations from the Christians of Rome.

Tychicus was also the bearer of the Epistle to the Church at Ephesus, and all these letters are supposed to have been written when St. Paul had been about a year at Rome.

To the Ephesians the Apostle speaks first of the many and great spiritual blessings received through Christ, Who is our peace. He prays that they may be strengthened by the Spirit of God, and exhorts them to fly from sin, to be united in "One Lord, one faith, one baptism." To these Ephesians, as to the Colossians, he speaks of the duties of the various relationships, and finally directs them to "Put on the armour of God," that they may resist in the evil day, when their wrestling would be against "the spirits of wickedness in high places."

The Church at Philippi had always shown a deep affection for the Apostle, and about this time they sent him a present as a mark of their love and sympathy for his sufferings.

When St. Paul wrote to thank them, he told them also about himself and that he expected soon to be tried, but that whether his sentence was life or death he should be content.

Probably about this same time was also written the Epistle to the Hebrews, which was addressed to the Jews of Judea and Jerusalem. In this letter the Apostle sets forth the immeasurable superiority of the New Law of Christ over the old Mosaic dispensation.

All this time the Christian Church at Rome was making rapid progress. With the zeal of St. Peter, and the eloquent teaching of St. Paul united in the great city, it was no wonder that the truth made its way even into the imperial court, for we find among the salutations of the Epistle to the Philippians, those of "Cæsar's household."

It was apparently through the influence of some of these more powerful disciples that, in the early part of the year 65, St. Paul was released from his imprisonment.

Very little information is given us in

the Scriptures respecting the Apostle after this liberation. We gain our knowledge chiefly from his own letters to Timothy and to Titus, and from the traditions of the early Church.

Thus it appears that the first use the Apostle made of his liberty was to undertake new missions, and to visit those Churches to which he had already preached "Christ crucified."

Though no longer young, he was still full of zeal for God's glory, and we find him now journeying to Spain, which he mentions in the Epistle to the Romans. A contemporary author—Clement of Rome—tells us that "Paul was the herald of the Christian faith to the whole world, and penetrated even to the limits of the West."

Accompanied by Titus, the Apostle also went into the island of Crete.

Taking a long voyage, he next visits Ephesus, passing thence to Macedonia. Titus had remained in Crete to watch over the newly founded Church, and with power to institute bishops and priests, and to him St. Paul writes an Epistle from Nicopolis, counselling him how to watch over the flock committed to his care. In this letter he speaks of remaining during the winter in this city, but he appears to have passed to Corinth, and thence to the Churches of Troas and Miletus, returning to Rome at the close of the year 66.

The first general persecution of the Church had commenced by order of Nero. Being disposed to give a spectacle which might rival the celebrated taking of Troy, this tyrant gave command for the city of Rome to be set on fire.

Rome was then composed of fourteen divisions, out of which only four escaped the flames of this tremendous conflagration. Nero, to excuse himself from the infamy of this act, laid the blame upon the Christians, and, as a punishment, had them arrested and condemned to the most dreadful torments.

Some were sewn up in the skins of wild beasts, and then were hunted by dogs in imitation of a barbarous chase. Many were crucified; others had their clothing smeared with some combustible material, and, fastened to posts in the streets or in the alleys of the imperial garden, were then set on fire.

During these horrors Nero walked, or drove in a car, about the gardens, or through the ruined city, enjoying the sufferings which his cruel nature had invented.

It was at the very height of this persecution that St. Paul was brought into Rome once more a prisoner, and dragged before the emperor. So great, however, were his courage and his eloquence, that he escaped any severer sentence than that of imprisonment. This time St. Paul was alone—his friends had removed to other parts, and feared to come to him. But, like that dear Saviour, Whose own disciples forsook Him in the hour of peril, St. Paul did not harshly censure his Christian brethren, but rather felt pity for their weakness of heart, and prayed that they might be forgiven for deserting him in his infirm age, with the near prospect of martyrdom before him.

While in prison, the Apostle wrote a second letter to Timothy, full of love and holy counsels. In this Epistle he exhorts him to "stir up the grace of God," which he had received at his ordination, and not to be discouraged by suffering.

He also utters a warning against those who have gone astray from truth, and concludes by speaking of his approaching death, and desires Timothy to come to him.

The trial of St. Paul terminated, as he had expected, with sentence of death.

In the midst of the fury of persecution, St. Peter had set no bounds to his zealous teaching of the faith of Christ. He had celebrated the Holy Mysteries in the house of a Christian named Pudens; in the presence of Nero himself he had confounded the audacious heresy of Simon Magus; he had converted, among others, a female slave greatly loved by the wicked emperor, and when she forsook the court, and served God by a virtuous life, the tyrant's rage against the Apostles of Christ broke out with fourfold strength. St. Peter was arrested and conveyed to the Mamertine prison, where he converted two of his guards to the Church.

Then together were these glorious Apostles brought before the governor of Rome, together they confessed the faith, and together were condemned to die.

A tradition of the early Church tells us that, before they died, the two Apostles prophesied the impending ruin of Jerusalem.

Then St. Peter—the Jew—was beaten with rods, and crucified with his head downwards upon Mount Janiculum, and buried in the Aurelian Way, near the temple of Apollo, the spot upon which the Vatican now stands.

St. Paul—the citizen of Rome—must not die by crucifixion but by the sword. Upon the same day, the 29th June, he, the old man of well-nigh seventy years, who had borne hunger and thirst, scourging, imprisonment, and chains, was led out beyond the gates of Rome to give up life for God.

In a place near the Fulvian waters, the crowd stayed their steps, and the executioner's sword severed the head of the old Apostle from his body. A beautiful legend tells us that three times that severed head leaped from the earth, and each time a clear fountain of water sprang up, to the amazement of all who witnessed the miracle.

There stands now upon that sacred spot the church of "Delle Tre Fontane," and visitors to the Eternal City, who go there to pray, have testified to the existence of these fountains.

In the story of the life of St. Paul, Apostle and Martyr, we see the marvellous effects of God's grace. It was by grace, through the strength of Christ, that he laboured so long, so faithfully, so successfully. It was by grace he had courage to endure hardness, and by grace that his heart thrilled with such fervent love to Christ—a love which sustained him through all the trials of his long life.

We read that St. Paul was exposed to one great trouble, a "thorn in the flesh," as Scripture terms it, and we are told that it was permitted for his humiliation. Three times he besought of God to take it from him, but the answer was, "My grace is sufficient for thee."

The Apostle had been highly educated; he was nobly born; he had received great intellectual gifts; he had gained knowledge and experience by travel into distant countries; he had even been caught up into paradise, and heard words which he could not utter, and seen wonders which it had been impossible to describe, yet God kept him humbled by some sharp and continued trial or temptation.

There are some who have imagined they could find in the life of St. Paul reasons for denying the teaching of our Holy Church, which affirms the supremacy of St. Peter.

St. Paul taught in words the unity of faith and discipline, the necessity of order, the obedience due to lawful authority, but he taught it also in his own life.

Glorious is his career; so marvellous in his conversion; so sublime in doctrine, so eloquent in teaching, so grandly successful in his missionary work, yet he comes to St. Peter as supreme head of the Church. To him he refers all matters of discipline, and to him he gives an account of his labours, because to him Christ said, " Thou art Peter, and upon this rock I will build my Church."

Nor are there wanting those who seek to prove from the writings of St. Paul, that to "believe in the Lord Jesus Christ " is salvation without the good works which the Church of Christ requires of her children.

The Apostle does indeed teach the

redemption of man through the death of Christ—that by grace and not through works are men justified. But he tells also just as plainly, just as clearly, of the necessity of a new life, of a casting away of sin; and while he says " There is now therefore no condemnation to them that are in Christ Jesus," he adds, "who walk not according to the flesh."

Profession of faith in Christ, but a corresponding holiness of life, a constant warfare against the world, the flesh, and the devil, the mortification of self, and of even sinless pleasures— this was the teaching of Paul the Apostle, as it is the teaching of Christ's Church.

Oh that we may receive some small measure of his burning love—love so humble, so faithful, so abiding. Oh that, like St. Paul, we too may become "new creatures in Jesus Christ," so that with him we may even dare to say, " Mihi vivere Christus est, et mori lucrum."

THE END.

R. WASHBOURNE'S CATALOGUE.

18 PATERNOSTER ROW, LONDON.

Post Office Orders to be made payable at the General Post Office.

The Feasts of Camelot, with the Tales that were told there. By Eleanora Louisa Hervey. 3s. 6d.

"This is really a very charming collection of tales, told as is evident from the title, by the Knights of the Round Table, at the Court of King Arthur. It is good for children and for grown up people too, to read these stories of knightly courtesy and adventure and of pure and healthy romance, and they have never been written in a more attractive style than by Mrs. Hervey in this little volume."—*Tablet.* "Elegant and imaginative invention, well selected language, and picturesque epithet."—*Athenæum.* "Full of chivalry and knightly deeds, not unmixed with touches of quaint humour."—*Court Journal.* "The substance and spirit of Arthurian romance."—*Examiner.* "A graceful and pleasing collection of stories."—*Daily News.* "Quaint and graceful little stories."—*Notes and Queries.* "To those who wish to go back to the prehistoric days and indulge themselves in the old dream-land of romance, this is just the book."—*Guardian.* "There is a high purpose in this charming book, one which is steadily pursued—it is the setting forth of the true meaning of chivalry."—*Morning Post.*

My Godmother's Stories from many Lands. By Eleanora Louisa Hervey. 12mo., 3s. 6d.

"One hundred and twenty stories, enchanting to youth, and interesting to a degree to those of more mature age."——"Without doubt the most engaging tales that we have had placed before us for many years."——"Children, aye, mothers, and those interested in the early years of childhood, will hail with delight the rich treasure Mrs. Hervey has placed before us."

The Story of the Life of St. Paul. By M. F. S., author of "Legends of the Saints," &c., &c. Fcap. 8vo., 2s. 6d. In the press.

A Hundred Years Ago; or, a Narrative of Events leading to the Marriage and Conversion to the Catholic Faith of Mr. and Mrs. Sidney, of Cowper Hall, Northumberland, to which are added a few other Incidents in their Life. By their Granddaughter. In the press.

Cassilda; or, the Moorish Princess of Toledo. 2s.

※ *Though this Catalogue does not contain many of the books of other Publishers, R. W. can supply all of them, no matter by whom they are published.*

Bertha; or, the Consequences of a Fault. 2s.
Captain Rougemont; the Miraculous Conversion. 2s.
The Little Hunchback. By the Countess de Ségur. With 8 full-page Illustrations. 3s.
The Irish Monthly. A Magazine containing several tales and interesting reading. Vol. 4, for 1876, 7s. 6d.; vols. 1 2 and 3, each, 7s. 6d.
The Franciscan Annals and Monthly Bulletin of the Third Order of S. Francis. Price 6d.
The Angelus. A Catholic Monthly Magazine, containing tales and other interesting reading. Price 2d.
Ritus Servandus in Expositione et Benedictione SS. 4to., red or purple cloth. 5s. 6d.
The Panegyrics of Fr. Segneri, S.J. Translated from the original Italian. With a preface by the Rev. Fr. W. Humphrey, S.J. In the press.
My Conversion and my Vocation. By Rev. Father Schouvaloff, Barnabite. In the press.
Spiritual Exercises according to the Method of S. Ignatius of Loyola. By Fr. Bellecius, S.J. 2s.
Albert the Great: his Life and Scholastic Labours. From original Documents. By Professor Sighart. Translated by Rev. Fr. T. A. Dixon, O.P. With a Photographic Portrait. 8vo., 10s. 6d.
Our Legends and Lives. A Gift for all Seasons. Poetry. By Eleanora Louisa Hervey. 6s.
Life of S. Patrick. By Miss Cusack. 6s.; gilt, 10s.
Mystical Flora of S. Francis de Sales, or the Christian Life under the Emblems of Plants. With coloured Illustrations. 8s.
Catholic Calendar for 1877, with Two Views of S. Etheldreda's Church, Ely Place, Holborn. 6d.
Legends of the Saints. By M. F. S., author of "Stories of the Saints." Square 16mo., 3s. 6d.
Stories of Martyr Priests. By M. F. S. 12mo., 3s. 6d.
The Three Wishes. A Tale. By M. F. S. 2s. 6d.
An Enquiry into the Nature and Results of Electricity and Magnetism. By Amyclanus. Illustrated. 6s. 6d.

Vespers and Benedictine Service. By Leopold de Prins.
A Devout Exposition of the Holy Mass; with an ample declaration of all the rites and ceremonies belonging to the same. By John Heigham, 1622. Edited by Austin Joseph Rowley, Priest. 12mo., 4s.
Life of Gregory Lopez, the Hermit. By Canon Doyle, O.S.B. With a Photograph. 12mo., 3s. 6d.
Road to Heaven. A game for family parties. 1s. With the Rules of the Game, bound, 2s.
Student's Handbook of British and American Literature. By Rev. O. L. Jenkins. 12mo., 8s.
The First Apostles of Europe; or the "Conversion of the Teutonic Race." By Mrs. Hope, author of "Early Martyrs," &c. 2 vols. 12mo., 10s.
Little Office of the Immaculate Conception. Translation approved by the Bishop of Clifton. 3d.
The Doctrine of Purgatory. By Rev. W. Marshall. 1s.
"This is unquestionably the best popular English treatise on this subject."—*Dublin Review*. "The evidence from passages of scripture amounts to proof the most incontestable."—*Tablet.* "This little treatise has astonished us by the amazing erudition which it compresses into so small a space, no less than by the irresistible cogency of the logic and the beauty of the style."—*Dolman's Magazine*.
The Serving Boy's Manual and Book of Public Devotions, containing all those prayers and devotions for Sundays and Holidays, usually divided in their recitation between the Priest and the Congregation. Compiled from approved sources, and adapted to Churches, served either by the Secular or the Regular Clergy. 32mo., embossed, 1s.; French morocco, 2s.; calf, 4s.; with Epistles and Gospels, 6d. extra.
First Communion Picture. Tastefully printed in gold and colours. Price 1s., or 9s. a dozen, *net*.
"Just what has long been wanted, a really good picture, with Tablet for First Communion and Confirmation."—*Tablet.*
Düsseldorf Gallery. This volume contains 357 Engravings, handsomely bound in half morocco, full gilt. Cash £5 5s. A smaller volume containing 134 Engravings (8vo. and large 8vo.), handsomely bound in half morocco, full gilt, £2 2s.

R. Washbourne, 18 Paternoster Row, London.

GARDEN OF THE SOUL.
(WASHBOURNE'S EDITION.)

Edited by the Rev. R. G. Davis. *With Imprimatur of the Cardinal-Archbishop.* Thirteenth Thousand. This Edition retains all the Devotions that have made the GARDEN OF THE SOUL, now for many generations, the well-known Prayer-book for English Catholics. During many years various Devotions have been introduced, and, in the form of appendices, have been added to other editions. These have now been incorporated into the body of the work, and, together with the Devotions to the Sacred Heart, to Saint Joseph, to the Guardian Angels, the Itinerarium, and other important additions, render this edition pre-eminently the Manual of Prayer, for both public and private use. The version of the Psalms has been carefully revised, and strictly conformed to the Douay translation of the Bible, published with the approbation of the LATE CARDINAL WISEMAN. The Forms of administering the Sacraments have been carefully translated, *as also the rubrical directions,* from the Ordo Administrandi Sacramenta. To enable all present, either at baptisms or other public administrations of the Sacraments, to pay due attention to the sacred rites, the Forms are inserted without any curtailment, both in Latin and English. The Devotions at Mass have been carefully revised, and enriched by copious adaptations from the prayers of the Missal. The preparation for the Sacraments of Penance and the Holy Eucharist have been the objects of especial care, to adapt them to the wants of those whose religious instruction may be deficient. Great attention has been paid to the quality of the paper and to the size of type used in the printing, to obviate that weariness so distressing to the eyes, caused by the use of books printed in small close type and on inferior paper.

"Garden of the Soul." Prices.

32mo. Embossed, 1s.; with rims and clasp, 1s. 6d.; with Epistles and Gospels, 1s. 6d.; with rims and clasps, 2s. French morocco, 2s.; with rims and clasp, 2s. 6d.; with E. and G., 2s. 6d.; with rims and clasp, 3s. French morocco extra gilt, 2s. 6d.; with rims and clasp, 3s.; with E. and G., 3s.; with rims and clasp, 3s. 6d. Calf, or morocco, 4s.; with rims and clasp, 5s. 6d.; with E. and G., 4s. 6d.; with rims and clasp, 6s. Calf or morocco extra gilt, 5s.; with rims and clasp, 6s. 6d.; with E. and G., 5s. 6d.; with rims and clasp, 7s. Velvet, with rims and clasp, 7s. 6d., 10s. 6d., and 13s.; with E. and G., 8s., 11s., and 13s. 6d. Russia, antique, with clasp, 10s., 12s. 6d.; with E. and G., 10s. 6d., 13s.; with corners and clasps, 20s.; with E. and G., 20s. 6d. Ivory, 14s., 16s., 20s., and 22s. 6d.; with E. and G., 14s. 6d., 16s. 6d., 20s. 6d., and 23s. Morocco antique, 10s.; with two patent clasps, 12s.; with E. and G., 10s. 6d. and 12s. 6d.; with corners and clasps, 18s.; with E. and G., 18s. 6d.

The Epistles and Gospels in cloth, 6d; roan, 1s. 6d.

"This is one of the best editions we have seen of one of the best of all our Prayer-books. It is well printed in clear large type, on good paper."—*Catholic Opinion.* "A very complete arrangement of this, which is emphatically the Prayer-book of every Catholic household. It is as cheap as it is good, and we heartily recommend it."—*Universe.* "Two striking features are the admirable order displayed throughout the book, and the insertion of the Indulgences, in small type, above Indulgenced Prayers."—*Weekly Register.*

The Little Garden of the Soul. 32mo. Cloth, 6d., with rims, 1s.; embossed, red edges, 9d., with rims 1s. 3d.; strong roan, 1s., with rims, 1s. 6d.; French morocco, 1s. 6d., with rims, 2s.; French morocco, extra gilt, 2s., with rims, 2s. 6d.; calf or morocco, 3s.; with rims, 4s.; calf or morocco, extra gilt, 4s.; with rims, 5s.; mor. antique, 7s. 6d., 10s. 6d. 12s. 16s.; velvet, with rims, 5s., 8s. 6d., 10s. 6d.; Russia, 5s.; with clasp, &c., 8s.; Russia antique, 17s. 6d.; ivory, with rims, 10s. 6d., 13s., 15s., 17s. 6d. Imitation ivory, with rims, 3s.; with oxydized silver or gilt mountings, in morocco case, 25s.

The Sacred Heart and St. Joseph.

Elevations to the Heart of Jesus. By Rev. Father Doyotte, S. J. Fcap. 8vo. 3s.

Paradise of God; or Virtues of the Sacred Heart. 4s.

Devotions to the Sacred Heart. By the Rev. S. Franco. 4s., paper covers, 2s.

Devotions to the Sacred Heart. By the Rev. J. Joy Dean. Fcap. 8vo. 3s.

Devotions to Sacred Heart of Jesus. By the Rt. Rev. Dr. Milner. *New Edition.* To which is added Devotions to the Immaculate Heart of Mary. 3d.; cloth, 6d.; gilt, 1s.

Sacred Heart of Jesus offered to the Piety of the Young engaged in Study. By Rev. A. Deham, S.J. 6d.

Pleadings of the Sacred Heart. By Rev. P. Comerford. 18mo. 1s.; gilt, 2s.; with the Handbook of the Confraternity, 1s. 6d.; Handbook, separately, 3d.

Treasury of the Sacred Heart. With Epistles and Gospels. 18mo. cloth, 3s. 6d.; roan, 4s. 6d. 32mo. 2s., roan 2s. 6d. calf 5s.; morocco, 6s.

Manual of Devotion to the Sacred Heart, from the Writings of Bl. Margaret Mary Alacoque. By Denys Casassayas. Translated. 3d.

Act of Consecration to the Sacred Heart. 1d.

Act of Reparation to the Sacred Heart. 1s. per 100.

The Power of St. Joseph. Meditations and Devotions. By Rev. Father Huguet. 18mo., 1s. 6d.

Novena of Meditations in Honour of S. Joseph, according to the method of S. Ignatius; preceded by a new exercise for hearing Mass according to the intentions of the souls in Purgatory. 18mo. 1s. 6d.

Novena to St. Joseph. Translated by M. A. Macdaniel. To which is added a Pastoral of the late Right Rev. Dr. Grant. 32mo. 4d.; cloth, 6d.

Devotions to St. Joseph. 1s. 2d. per 100, post free.

Litany of S. Joseph, &c. 1s. 2d. per 100, post free.

In Suffragiis Sanctorum. Commem S. Josephi. Commem S. Georgii. Set of five for 4d.

Religious Reading.

"Vitis Mystica;" or, the True Vine. A Treatise on the Passion of Our Lord. From the Latin. By the Rev. W. R. Bernard Brownlow. With Frontispiece. 18mo. 4s., red edges, 4s. 6d.

<small>"It is a pity that such a beautiful treatise should for so many centuries have remained untranslated into our tongue."—*Tablet.*
"An excellent translation of a beautiful treatise."—*Dublin Review.*</small>

The Sufferings of our Lord Jesus Christ. Preached in London by Father Claude de la Colombière, S. J., in the Chapel Royal, St. James's, in the year 1677. 18mo. 1s. and 1s. 6d.; red edges, 2s.

Lenten Thoughts. Drawn from the Gospel for each day in Lent. By the Bishop of Northampton. 2s.; red edges, 2s. 6d.

The Happiness of Heaven. By a Father of the Society of Jesus. Fcap. 8vo. 4s.

God our Father. By the same Author. Fcap. 8vo. 4s.

Holy Places; their Sanctity and Authenticity. By the Rev. Fr. Philpin. With Maps. Crown 8vo. 6s.

<small>Fr. Philpin weighs the comparative value of extraordinary, ordinary, and natural evidence, and gives an admirable summary of the witness of the early centuries regarding the holy places of Jerusalem, with archæological and architectural proofs. It is a complete treatise of the subject."—*The Month.* "The author treats his subject with a thorough system, and a competent knowledge. It is a book of singular attractiveness and considerable merit."—*Church Herald.*
"Dean Stanley and other sinners in controversy are treated with great gentleness. They are indeed thoroughly exposed and refuted."—*Register.* "Fr. Philpin has a particularly nervous and fresh style of handling his subject, with an occasional picturesqueness of epithet or simile."—*Tablet.*</small>

The Consoler; or, Pious Readings addressed to the Sick and to all who are afflicted. By Lambilotte. Translated by the Right Rev. Abbot Burder. Fcp. 8vo. 4s. 6d., red edges, 5s.

<small>"Written in plain and simple language, it is very specially adapted for one of the subjects which its writer had in view, namely, its introduction into hospitals."—*Tablet.* "A work replete with wise comfort for every affliction."—*Universe.* "A spiritual treatise of great beauty and value."—*Church Herald.*</small>

Confidence in the Mercy of God. By Mgr. Languet. Translated by Abbot Burder. 3s.

Easy Way to God. By Cardinal Bona. Translated by Father Collins. Fcap. 8vo. 3s.

The Selva, or a Collection of Matter for Sermons. By St. Liguori. 5s.

The Souls in Purgatory. By Abbot Burder, 3d.

"It will be found most useful as an aid to the cultivation of this especial devotion."—*Register.*

Novena in favour of the Souls in Purgatory. By Abbé Serre. Translated by Abbot Burder, 3d.

Flowers of Christian Wisdom. By Lucien Henry. With a Preface by the Right Hon. Lady Herbert of Lea. 18mo. 2s.; red edges, 2s. 6d.

"A compilation of some of the most beautiful thoughts and passages in the works of the Fathers, the great schoolmen, and eminent modern Churchmen."—*Church Times.* "It is a compilation of gems of thought, carefully selected."—*Tablet.* "It is a small but exquisite bouquet, like that which S. Francis of Sales has prepared for *Philothea.*"—*Universe.*

Alzog's Universal Church History. Translated by Pabisch and Byrne. 8vo., 3 Vols., each 20s.

A General History of the Catholic Church: from the commencement of the Christian Era until the present time. By Abbé Darras. 4 vols., 48s.

The Book of Perpetual Adoration; or, the Love of Jesus in the most Holy Sacrament of the Altar. By Mgr. Boudon. Edited by the Rev. J. Redman, D.D. Fcap. 8vo. 3s.; red edges, 3s. 6d.

"One of Boudon's most beautiful works."—*Tablet.* "The devotions at the end will be very acceptable aids in visiting the Blessed Sacrament."—*The Month.* "It has been pronounced to be 'the most beautiful of all books written in honour of the Blessed Sacrament.'"—*The Nation.*

Before the Altar. Two short Meditations. 6d.

Ebba; or, the Supernatural Power of the Blessed Sacrament. In French. 12mo. 1s. 6d.; cloth gilt, 2s. 6d.

Apostleship of Prayer. By Rev. H. Ramière. 6s.

Spiritual Works of Louis of Blois, Abbot of Liesse. Edited by the Rev. John Edward Bowden, of the Oratory. Fcap. 8vo. 3s. 6d; red edges, 4s.

"No more important or welcome addition could have been made to our English ascetical literature than this little book. It is a model of good translation."—*Dublin Review.* "Elegant and flowing."—*Register.* "Most useful of meditations."—*Catholic Opinion.*

Heaven Opened by the Practice of Frequent Confession and Communion. By the Abbé Favre. Translated from the French, carefully revised by a Father of the Society of Jesus. Third Edition. Fcap. 8vo. 3s. 6d. ; red edges, 4s. Cheap edit. 2s.

"This beautiful little book of devotion. We may recommend it to the clergy as well as to the laity."—*Tablet.* "It is filled with quotations from the Holy Scriptures, the Fathers, and the Councils of the Church, and thus will be found of material assistance to the clergy, as a storehouse of doctrinal and ascetical authorities on the two great sacraments of Holy Eucharist and Penance."—*Register.*

The Spiritual Life.—Conferences delivered to the *Enfants de Marie* by Père Ravignan. Cr. 8vo. 5s.

"Ladies could not have a better book for their spiritual reading."—*Tablet.* "A depth of eloquence and power of exhortation which few living preachers can rival."—*Church Review.*

The Supernatural Life. Translated from the French of Mgr. Mermillod, with a Preface by Lady Herbert. Cr. 8vo. 5s.

Spiritual Conferences on the Mysteries of Faith and the Interior Life. By Father Collins. 4s.

- **The Eucharist and the Christian Life.** By Mgr. de la Bouillerie. Translated. Fcap. 8vo. 3s. 6d.

Holy Communion : it is my Life. By H. Lebon. 4s.

The Blessed Sacrament of the Miracle. 10 Photographs. Price 2s. 6d.

On Contemporary Prophecies. By Mgr. Dupanloup. Translated by Rev. Dr. Redmond. 8vo. 1s.

Good Thoughts for Priests and People; or Short Meditations for Every Day in the Year. By Rev. T. Noethen. 12mo. 8s.

One Hundred Pious Reflections. Extracted from Alban Butler's "Lives of the Saints." 18mo. cloth, red edges, 2s. ; cheap edition, 1s.

"A happy idea. The author of 'The Lives of the Saints' had a way of breathing into his language the unction and force which carries the truth of the Gospel into the heart."—*Letter to the Editor from* THE RIGHT REV. DR. ULLATHORNE.

Some Documents concerning the Association of Prayers, in Honour of Mary Immaculate, for the Return of the Greek-Russian Church to Catholic Unity. By the Rev. C. Tondini. 3d.

Following of Christ. Small pocket edition, 1s. cloth; 1s. 6d. embossed; roan, 2s.; French morocco, 2s. 6d.; calf or morocco, 4s. 6d.; calf or morocco extra gilt, 5s. 6d.; ivory, 15s. and 16s.; morocco, antique, 17s. 6d.; russia antique, 20s.

The Imitation of Christ. With reflections. 32mo. 1s. Persian calf, 3s. 6d. Also an Edition with ornamental borders. Fcap. cloth, red edges, 3s. 6d.; morocco, 10s. 6d.; morocco antique, 25s.

The Apostles of Europe: or, the Conversion of the Teutonic Race. By Mrs. Hope, author of "Early Martyrs." Edited by the Rev. Father Dalgairns. 2 vols. crown 8vo. 10s.

"It is good in itself, possessing considerable literary merit; it forms one of the few Catholic books brought out in this country which are not translations or adaptations."—*Dublin Review.* "It is a great thing to find a writer of a book of this class so clearly grasping, and so boldly setting forth, truths which, familiar as they are to scholars, are still utterly unknown by most of the writers of our smaller literature."—*Saturday Review.* "A very valuable work . . . . Mrs. Hope has compiled an original history, which gives constant evidence of great erudition, and sound historical judgment."—*Month.* "This is a most taking book: it is solid history and romance in one."—*Catholic Opinion.* "It is carefully, and in many parts beautifully written."—*Universe.*

Contemplations on the Most Holy Sacrament of the Altar, drawn from the Sacred Scriptures. 18mo. cloth, 2s.; cloth extra, red edges, 2s. 6d.

"This is a welcome addition to our books of Scriptural devotion. It contains thirty-four excellent subjects of reflection before the Blessed Sacrament, or for making a spiritual visit to the Blessed Sacrament at home; for the use of the sick."—*Dublin Review.*

Cistercian Order: its Mission and Spirit. Comprising the Life of S. Robert of Newminster, and S. Robert of Knaresborough. By Fr. Collins. 3s. 6d.

Cistercian Legends of the 13th Century. Translated from the Latin by the Rev. Henry Collins. 3s.

"Interesting records of Cistercian sanctity and cloistral experience."—*Dublin Review.* "A casquet of jewels."—*Weekly Register.* "Most beautiful legends, full of deep spiritual reading."—*Tablet.* "Anecdotes, full of heavenly wisdom."—*Catholic Opinion.*

The Soul united to Jesus in the Adorable Sacrament. 1s. 6d.

The Dove of the Tabernacle. By Fr. Kinane. 1s. 6d.

R. Washbourne, 18 Paternoster Row, London.

Spalding's (Archbp.) Works. Miscellanea, 2 vols., 21s.; Protestant Reformation, 2 vols., 21s.; Evidences of Catholicity, 10s. 6d.

The Directorium Asceticum; or Guide to the Spiritual Life. By Scaramelli. Translated and edited at St. Beuno's College. 4 vols. crown 8vo. 24s.

Maxims of the Kingdom of Heaven. New and enlarged Edition. 5s.; red edges, 5s. 6d.; calf or morocco, 10s. 6d.

"Most suitable for meditation and reference."—*Dublin Review.*

Balmes' Letters to a Sceptic on Matters of Religion. 6s.

Thy Gods, O Israel. A Picture in Verse of the Religious Anomalies of our Time. Cr. 8vo. 2s.

BY ARTHUR AND T. W. M. MARSHALL.

Comedy of Convocation in the English Church. Edited by Archdeacon Chasuble, D.D. 2s. 6d.

The Oxford Undergraduate of Twenty Years Ago: his Religion, his Studies, his Antics. By a Bachelor of Arts. 2s. 6d.; cloth, 3s. 6d.

"The writing is full of brilliancy and point."—*Tablet.* "It will deservedly attract attention, not only by the briskness and liveliness of its style, but also by the accuracy of the picture which it probably gives of an individual experience."—*The Month.*

The Infallibility of the Pope. A Lecture. By the Author of "The Oxford Undergraduate." 8vo. 1s.

"A splendid lecture, by one who thoroughly understands his subject, and in addition is possessed of a rare power of language in which to put before others what he himself knows so well."—*Universe.* "There are few writers so well able to make things plain and intelligible as the author of 'The Comedy of Convocation.'. . . The lecture is a model of argument and style."—*Register.*

Reply to the Bishop of Ripon's Attack on the Catholic Church. By the same Author. 6d.

The English Religion. Letters addressed to an Irish Gentleman. By A. M. 1s.

The Harmony of Anglicanism. Report of a Conference on Church Defence. 8vo. 2s. 6d.

"'Church Defence' is characterized by the same caustic irony, the same good-natured satire, the same logical acuteness which distinguished its predecessor, the 'Comedy of Convocation.'. . . A more scathing bit of irony we have seldom met with."—*Tablet.* "Clever, humorous, witty, learned, written by a keen but sarcastic observer of the Establishment, it is calculated to make defenders wince as much as it is to make all others smile."—*Nonconformist.*

R. Washbourne, 18 Paternoster Row, London.

The Roman Question. By Dr. Husenbeth. 6d.
Consoling Thoughts of St. Francis de Sales. 2s.
Holy Readings. Short Selections from well-known Authors. By J. R. Digby Beste, Esq. 32mo. cloth, 2s.; cloth, red edges, 2s. 6d.; roan, 3s.; morocco, 6s. [See "Catholic Hours," p. 23.]
Anti-Janus. By Hergenröther. Translated by Professor Robertson. 6s.
St. Peter; his Name and his Office as set forth in Holy Scripture. By T. W. Allies. *Second Edition.* Revised. Crown 8vo. 5s.

"A standard work. There is no single book in English, on the Catholic side, which contains the Scriptural argument about St. Peter and the Papacy so clearly or conclusively put."—*Month.*

Sancti Alphonsi Doctoris Officium Parvum—Novena and Little Office in honour of St. Alphonsus. Fcap. 8vo. 1s.; cloth, 2s.; cloth extra, 3s.
The Life of Pleasure. Translated from the French of Mgr. Dechamps. Fcap. 8vo. 1s. 6d.
Sure Way to Heaven: a little Manual for Confession and Holy Communion. 32mo. cloth, 6d. Persian 2s. 6d. Calf or morocco, 3s. 6d.
Compendium of the History of the Catholic Church. By Rev. T. Noethen. 12mo. 8s.
History of the Catholic Church, for schools. By Rev. T. Noethen. 12mo. 5s. 6d.
The Rule of our most holy Father St. Benedict, Patriarch of Monks. From the old English edition of 1638. Edited by one of the Benedictine Fathers of St. Michael's, near Hereford. Fcap. 8vo. 4s. 6d.
Catholic Calendar and Church Guide. Price 6d.
Catholic Directory for Scotland. 1s.
Protestantism and Liberty. By Professor Ozanam. Translated by W. C. Robinson. 8vo. 1s.
Catholicism, Liberalism, and Socialism. Translated from the Spanish of Donoso Cortes, by Rev. W. M'Donald. 6s.
The Jesuits, and other Essays. By Willis Nevin. Fcap. 8vo., 1s. 6d.

Meditations on the Life of Our Lord. By Rev. J. Nouet, S.J. 2 vols., 7s. 6d.

The Tradition of the Syriac Church of Antioch, concerning the Primacy and Prerogatives of S. Peter, and of his successors, the Roman Pontiffs. By the Most Rev. C. B. Benni. 8vo., 7s. 6d.

Dr. Pusey's Eirenicon considered in Relation to Catholic Unity. By H. N. Oxenham. 2s. 6d.

Familiar Instructions on Christian Truths. By a Priest. No. 1, Detraction. 4d. No. 2, The Dignity of the Priesthood. 3d. No. 3, Necessity of hearing the Word of God. Why it produces no fruit, and how to be heard. On the necessity of Faith. 3d.

Sweetness of Holy Living; or Honey culled from the Flower Garden of S. Francis of Sales. 1s. French morocco, 3s.

"In it will be found some excellent aids to devotion and meditation."—*Weekly Register*.

Père Lacordaire's Conferences. God, 6s. Jesus Christ, 6s. God and Man, 6s. Life, 6s.

Commonitory of S. Vincent of Lerins. 12mo. 1s. 3d.

Men and Women of the English Reformation, from the days of Wolsey to the death of Cranmer. By S. H. Burke, M.A. Vol. ii., 6s. 6d.

The chief topics of importance in the second volume are: Archbishop Cranmer's opinions upon Confession; The Religious Houses of Olden England; Burnet as a Historian; What were Lord Cromwell's Religious Sentiments? Effects of the Confiscation on the People; The Church and the Holy Scriptures; Death-bed Horrors of Henry VIII.; Scenes upon the Scaffold—Lady Jane Grey's heroic Death; The Rack and the Stake; The Archbishop condemned to be Burnt Alive—Awful Scene; A General View of Cranmer's Life.

A Devout Paraphrase on the Seven Penitential Psalms; or, a Practical Guide to Repentance. By the Rev. Fr. Blyth. To which is added :—Necessity of Purifying the Soul, by St. Francis of Sales. 18mo., 1s. 6d.; red edges, 2s.; cheap edition, 1s.

"A new edition of a book well known to our grandfathers The work is full of devotion and of the spirit of prayer."—*Universe*.

A New Miracle at Rome; through the Intercession of Blessed John Berchmans. 2d.

Cure of Blindness; through the Intercession of Our Lady and St. Ignatius. 2d.

Sanctuary Meditations for Priests and Frequent Communicants. Translated from the original Spanish of Father Baltasar Gracian, S.J., 1669. By Mariana Monteiro. Fcap. 8vo., 4s.
A Homely Discourse. Mary Magdalen. Cr. 8vo. 6d.
Extemporaneous Speaking. By Rev. T. J. Potter. 5s.
Pastor and People. By Rev. T. J. Potter. 5s.
Eight Short Sermon Essays. By Dr. Redmond. 1s.
One Hundred Short Sermons. By Canon Thomas. 12s.
Catholic Sermons. By Father Burke, and others. 2s.
The Light of the Holy Spirit in the World. Sermons by Bishop Hedley, O.S.B. 1s.; cloth, 1s. 6d.
Sermon at the Month's Mind of the Most Rev. Dr. Spalding, Archbishop of Baltimore. 1s.
The Church of England and its Defenders. By the Rev. W. R. Bernard Brownlow. 8vo. 1s. 6d.
Lectures on the Life, Writings, and Times of Edmund Burke. By Professor Robertson. 3s. 6d.
Professor Robertson's Lectures on Modern History and Biography. Crown 8vo. cloth, 6s.
The Knight of the Faith. By the Rev. Dr. Laing.
1. A Favourite Fallacy about Private Judgment. 1d.
2. Catholic not Roman Catholic. 4d.
3. Rationale of the Mass. 1s.
4. Challenge to the Churches. 1d.
5. Absurd Protestant Opinions. 4d.
6. Whence the Monarch's right to rule. 2s. 6d.
7. Protestantism against the Natural Moral Law. 1d.
8. What is Christianity? 6d.
Explanation of the Medal or Cross of S. Benedict. 1d.
Diary of a Confessor of the Faith. 12mo. 1s.
Sursum, 1s. Homeward, 2s. Both by Rev. Fr. Rawes.
Commentary on the Psalms. By Bellarmin. 4to. 6s.

BY SISTER M. F. CLARE.

Woman's Work in Modern Society. 4s. 6d.
A Nun's Advice to her Girls. 2s. 6d.
Daily Steps to Heaven. Fcap. 8vo. 4s. 6d.
Book of the Blessed Ones. 4s. 6d.
Jesus and Jerusalem; or, the Way Home. 4s. 6d.

Exposition of the Epistles of St. Paul. By the Right Rev. Dr. MacEvilly. 2 vols. 18s.
An Exposition of the Gospels. By the Right Rev. Dr. MacEvilly. Vol. i., 12s. 6d.
Monastic Legends. By E. G. K. Browne. 8vo. 6d.
A Few Words from Lady Mildred's Housekeeper. 2d.
"The good advice of an experienced upper servant on such subjects ought not to fall on unwilling ears."—*Register.*

BY HIS EMINENCE CARDINAL MANNING.
Confraternity of the Holy Family. 8vo. 3d.
Confidence in God. 1s.
The Convocation in Crown and Council. 6d.
Temporal Sovereignty of the Popes. 1s. ; cloth, 1s. 6d.
The Church, the Spirit, and the Word. 6d.

BY THE PASSIONIST FATHERS.
The Mirror of Faith : your Likeness in it. 3s.
The School of Jesus Crucified. 5s.
The Manual of the Cross and Passion. 32mo. 2s. 6d.
The Manual of the Seven Dolours. 32mo. 1s. 6d.
The Christian Armed. 32mo. 1s. 6d.
Guide to Sacred Eloquence. 2s.

Religious Instruction.

The Catechism of Christian Doctrine. Approved for the use of the Faithful in all the Dioceses of England and Wales. Price 1d. ; cloth, 2d.
The Catechism, Illustrated with Passages from the Holy Scriptures. Arranged by the Rev. J. B. Bagshawe, with Imprimatur. Crown 8vo. 2s. 6d.
"I believe the Catechism to be one of the best possible books of controversy, to those, at least, who are inquiring with a real desire to find the truth."—*Extract from the Preface.*
"An excellent idea. The very thing of all others that is needed by many under instruction."—*Tablet.* "It is a book which will do incalculable good. Our priests will hail with pleasure so valuable a help to their weekly instructions in the Catechism, while in schools its value will be equally recognized."—*Weekly Register.*
A First Sequel to the Catechism. By the Rev. J. Nary. 32mo. 1d.
Catechism made Easy. A Familiar Explanation of "The Catechism of Christian Doctrine." By Rev. H. Gibson. Vol. I., 4s. Vol. II., 4s.

The Threshold of the Catholic Church. A course of Plain Instructions for those entering her Communion. By Rev. J. B. Bagshawe. Cr. 8vo. 4s.

"A scholarly, well-written book, full of information."—*Church Herald.* "An admirable book, which will be of infinite service to thousands."—*Universe.* "Plain, practical, and unpretentious, it exhausts so entirely the various subjects of instruction necessary for our converts, that few missionary priests will care to dispense with its assistance."—*Register.* "It has very special merits of its own. . It is the work, not only of a thoughtful writer and good theologian, but of a wise and experienced priest."—*Dublin Review.* "Its characteristic is the singular simplicity and clearness with which everything is explained. . . It will save priests hours and days of time."—*Tablet.* "There was a great want of a manual of instruction for convents, and the want has now been supplied, and in the most satisfactory manner."—*The Month.*

A General Catechism of the Christian Doctrine. By the Right Rev. Dr. Poirier. 18mo. 9d.

Frassinetti's Dogmatic Catechism. Translated by the Oblate Fathers of St. Charles. 3s.

"We give a few extracts from Frassinetti's work, as samples of its excellent execution."—*Dublin Review.* "Needs no commendation."—*Month.* "It will be found useful, not only to catechists, but also for the instruction of converts."—*Tablet.*

Mgr. de Ségur's Books for Little Children. Translated. Confession; Holy Communion; Child Jesus; Piety; Prayer; Temptation. 3d. each.

The Seven Sacraments explained and defended. Edited by a Catholic Clergyman. 1s. 6d.

The Christian Instructed in the nature and use of Indulgences. By Rev. F. A. Maurel, S.J. 3s.

Protestant Principles Examined by the Written Word. Originally entitled, "The Protestant's Trial by the Written Word." *New edition.* 18mo. 1s.

"An excellent book."—*Church News.* "A good specimen of the concise controversial writing of English Catholics in the early part of the seventeenth century."—*Catholic Opinion.* "A little book which might be consulted profitably by any Catholic."—*Church Times.* "A clever little manual."—*Westminster Gazette.* "A useful little volume."—*The Month.* "An excellent little book."—*Weekly Register.* "A well-written and well-argued treatise."—*Tablet.*

Dr. Butler's *First* Catechism, ½d. *Second* Catechism, 1d.; *Third* Catechism, 1½d.

Dr. Doyle's Catechism, 1½d.

Lessons on the Christian Doctrine, 1½d.

Descriptive Guide to the Mass. By the Rev. Dr. Laing. 1s.; extra cloth, 1s. 6d.
"An attempt to exhibit the structure of the Mass. The logical relation of parts is ingeniously effected by an elaborate employment of differences of type, so that the classification, down to the minutest subdivision, may at once be caught by the eye."—*Tablet.*

The Necessity of Enquiry as to Religion. By Henry John Pye, M.A. 4d.; cloth, 6d.
"Mr. Pye is particularly plain and straightforward."—*Tablet.*
"It is calculated to do much good. We recommend it to the clergy, and think it a most useful work to place in the hands of all who are under instruction."—*Westminster Gazette.*

The Grounds of Catholic Doctrine. By Dr. Challoner. Large type edition. 18mo. cloth, 4d.

Fleury's Historical Catechism. Large edition, 1½d.

Bible History for the use of Catholic Schools and Families. By the Rev. R. Gilmour. 2s.

Origin and Progress of Religious Orders, and Happiness of a Religious State. By Fr. J. Platus, S. J. 2s. 6d.

Children of Mary in the World. 32mo. 1d.

Christian Politeness. By the Ven. de la Salle. 1s.

Duties of a Christian. By the Ven. de la Salle. 2s.

The Young Catholic's Guide to Confession and Holy Communion. By Dr. Kenny. *Third edition.* Paper, 4d.; cloth, 6d.; cloth, red edges, 9d.

Instructions for the Sacrament of Confirmation. 6d.

Auricular Confession. By Rev. Dr. Melia. 1s. 6d.

Goffine's Explanation of the Epistles and Gospels. 7s.

Rules for a Christian Life. By S. Charles Borromeo. 2d.

Anglican Orders. By Canon Williams. 3s. 6d.

The Monks of Iona and the Duke of Argyll. By the Rev. J. Stewart M'Corry, D.D. 8vo. 3s. 6d.

The Child. By Mgr. Dupanloup. Translated, 3s. 6d.

The Penny Bank. By the Rev. Fr. Richardson. 1d.

The Crusade, or Catholic Association for the Suppression of Drunkenness. By the same. 1d.

The Catholic Total Abstinence League of the Cross. By the same. 1d. each; or 6s. for 144, *net.*

Holy War, by the same, 1d.; Cross, 2d.

Catholic Sick and Benefit Club; or, the Guild of our Lady, and St. Joseph's Burial Society. By the Rev. Fr. Richardson. 32mo. 4d. Burial Society by itself, 2d.

Dramas, Comedies, Farces.

St. William of York. A Drama in Two Acts, for boys. 6d.
Major John André. An Historical Drama (Boys.) 2s.
He would be a Lord. Comedy in Three Acts. (Boys.) 2s.
St. Louis in Chains. Drama in Five Acts, for boys. 2s.
The Expiation. A Drama in Three Acts, for boys. 2s.
Shandy Maguire. A Farce for boys in Two Acts. 1s.
The Duchess Transformed. A Comedy in One Act, for girls. By W. H. A. 6d.
The Reverse of the Medal. A Drama in Four Acts, for young ladies. 6d.
Ernscliff Hall: or, Two Days Spent with a Great-Aunt. A Drama in Three Acts, for young ladies. 6d.
Filiola. A Drama in Four Acts, for young ladies. 6d.
The Convent Martyr. By Dr. Husenbeth. 2s.
Road to Heaven. A game for family parties, 1s. & 2s.
Shakespeare. Expurgated edition, 6s. Comedies, 3s. 6d.

Lives of Saints, &c.

Lives of the Saints for every Day in the Year. Translated from M. Didot's edition. Beautifully printed on thick toned paper, with borders from ancient sources, scarlet cloth gilt, gilt edges, 4to. 16s.
Lives of the First Religious of the Visitation of Holy Mary. By Mother Frances Magdalen de Chaugy. With two Photographs. 2 vols., cr. 8vo. 12s.
S. Vincent Ferrer, of the Order of Friar Preachers: his Life, Spiritual Teaching, and practical Devotion. By Fr. Pradel. Translated by Fr. Dixon, O.P. With a Photograph. 5s.
Butler's Lives of the Saints. 2 vols., 8vo., cloth, 28s.; or in cloth gilt, 34s.; or in 4 vols., 8vo., cloth, 32s.; or in cloth gilt, 48s.; or in leather gilt, 64s.
Oratorian Lives of the Saints. Second Series. Post 8vo.
S. Bernardine of Siena. With a portrait, 5s.
S. Philip Benizi. With a portrait, 5s.
S. Veronica Giuliani, and Blessed Battista Varani. With a portrait, 5s.
S. John of God. With a portrait, 5s.

Life of Sister Mary Cherubina Clare of S. Francis, Translated from the Italian, with Preface by Lady Herbert. Cr. 8vo. with Photograph, 3s. 6d.
Stories of the Saints. By M. F S., author of "Tom's Crucifix, and other Tales," "Catherine Hamilton," &c. 2 vols., each 3s. 6d., gilt, 4s. 6d.
Stories of Holy Lives. By M. F. S. Fcp. 8vo., 3s. 6d.
Life of B. Giovanni Colombini. By Feo Belcari. Translated from the editions of 1541 and 1832. with a Photograph. Cr. 8vo. 3s. 6d.
Sketch of the Life and Letters of the Countess Adelstan. By E. A. M., author of "Rosalie, or the Memoirs of a French Child," "Life of Paul Seigneret, &c." 2s. 6d.
Life and Prophecies of S. Columbkille, 3s. 6d.
New Model for Youth; or, Life of Richard Aloysius Pennefather. 3s. 6d.
Recollections of Cardinal Wiseman, &c. By M. J. Arnold. 2s. 6d.
Life of St. Augustine of Canterbury. 12mo. 3s. 6d.
Life of St. German. 12mo. cloth, 3s. 6d.
Life of Stephen Langton. 12mo. cloth, 2s. 6d.
Prince and Saviour. A Life of Christ for the Young. By Rosa Mulholland. 6d. Illustrated, 2s. 6d.
The First Christmas for our dear little ones. By Miss Mulholland. 15 Illustrations, 4to. 5s.
S. Paul of the Cross. By the Passionist Fathers. 2s. 6d.
Nano Nagle. By Rev. W. Hutch, D.D. 7s. 6d.
Life of St. Boniface. By Mrs. Hope. 6s.
"Every one knows the story of S. Boniface's martyrdom, but every one has not heard it so stirringly set forth as in her 22nd chapter by Mrs. Hope."—*Dublin Review.*
Life of the Ven. Anna Maria Taigi. From the French of Calixte, by A. V. Smith Sligo. 5s.
Venerable Mary Christina of Savoy. 6d.
Memoirs of a Guardian Angel. Fcap. 8vo. 4s.
St. Patrick, the Apostle of Ireland. 1s.
Life of St. Patrick. 12mo. 1s.; 8vo., 6s.; gilt, 10s.
Life of St. Bridget, and of other Saints of Ireland. 1s.
Insula Sanctorum: the Island of Saints. 1s.; cloth, 2s.

R. Washbourne, 18 *Paternoster Row, London.*

Sufferings of Our Lord. With Introduction by Dr. Husenbeth. Illustrated. 5s.
Harmony of the Passion of Our Lord. In English and French. By Madame Paul Gayrard. 1s. 6d.
Life, Passion, Death, and Resurrection of Our Blessed Lord. Translated from Ribadeneira. 1s.
Life of Paul Seigneret, Seminarist of Saint-Sulpice. Fcap. 8vo., 1s.; cloth extra, 1s. 6d.; gilt, 2s.
"An affecting and well-told narrative... It will be a great favourite, especially with our pure-minded, high-spirited young people."—*Universe.* "We commend it to parents with sons under their care, and especially do we recommend it to those who are charged with the education and training of our Catholic youth."—*Register.*

A Daughter of St. Dominic. By Grace Ramsay. Fcap. 8vo. 1s. 6d.; cloth extra, 2s.
"A beautiful little work. The narrative is highly interesting."—*Dublin Review.* "It is full of courage and faith and Catholic heroism."—*Universe.* "A beautiful picture of the wonders effected by ubiquitous charity, and still more by fervent prayer."—*Tablet.*

Glory of St. Vincent de Paul. By Cardinal Manning. 1s.
Life of S. Edmund of Canterbury. From the French of the Rev. Father Massé, S. J. 1s. and 1s. 6d.
Life of St. Francis of Assisi. From the Italian of St. Bonaventure. By Miss Lockhart. 3s. 6d.; 4s. gilt.
Life of Fr. de Ravignan. Crown 8vo. 9s.
The Pilgrimage to Paray le Monial. 6d.
Patron Saints. By Eliza Allen Starr. Cr. 8vo. 10s.
His Eminence Cardinal Wiseman; with full account of his Obsequies. 1s.; cloth, 1s. 6d.
Count de Montalembert. By George White. 6d.
Life of Mgr. Weedall. By Dr. Husenbeth. 1s.
Life of Pope Pius IX. 6d. Cheap edition, 1d.
Challoner's Memoirs of Missionary Priests. 8vo. 6s.

BY SISTER MARY FRANCES CLARE.

O'Connell: his Life and Times. 2 vols., 18s.
The Liberator: his Speeches and Letters. 2 vols., 18s.
Life of Father Matthew. 2s. 6d.
Life of Mary O'Hagan, Abbess, Poor Clares. 6s.
Life of St. Aloysius. 6d.; St. Joseph, 6d., cloth, 1s.; St. Patrick, 6d., cloth, 1s.; 8vo., 6s.; gilt, 10s.
Life of St. Patrick. Illustrated by Doyle. 4to. 20s.

R. Washbourne, 18 Paternoster Row, London.

Our Lady.

Regina Sæculorum, or, Mary venerated in all Ages. Devotions to the Blessed Virgin from ancient sources. Fcap. 8vo. 3s.

Readings for the Feasts of Our Lady, and especially for the Month of May. By the Rev. A. P. Bethell. 18mo. 1s. 6d. ; cheap edition, 1s.

The History of the Blessed Virgin. By the Abbé Orsini. Translated by Dr. Husenbeth. With eight Illustrations. Crown 8vo. 3s. 6d.

The Path of Mary. By one of her loving children. 1s.

Manual of Devotions in Honour of Our Lady of Sorrows. Compiled by the Clergy at St. Patrick's Soho. 18mo. 1s. ; cloth, red edges, 1s. 6d.

Our Blessed Lady of Lourdes: a Faithful Narrative of the Apparitions of the Blessed Virgin. By F. C. Husenbeth, D.D. 18mo. 6d. ; cloth, 1s.; with Novena, 1s. ; cloth, 1s. 6d. Novena, separately, 4d. ; Litany, 1d., or 6s. per 100.

Devotion to Our Lady in North America. By the Rev. Xavier Donald Macleod. 8vo. 7s. 6d.

"The work of an author than whom few more gifted writers have ever appeared among us. It is not merely a religious work, but it has all the charms of an entertaining book of travels. We can hardly find words to express our high admiration of it."—*Weekly Register.*

Letters to my God-Child. On the Veneration of the Blessed Virgin. By Mrs. Stuart Laidlaw. 4d.

Life of the Ever-Blessed Virgin. Proposed as a Model to Christian Women. 1s.

The Blessed Virgin's Root traced in the Tribe of Ephraim. By the Rev. Dr. Laing. 8vo. 10s. 6d.

Litany of the Seven Dolours. 1d. each, or 6s. per 100.

Month of Mary for all the Faithful. By Rev. P. Comerford. 1s.

Month of Mary for Interior Souls. By M. A. Macdaniel. 18mo. 2s.

Month of Mary, principally for the use of religious communities. 18mo. 1s. 6d.

Mariæ Lauretana; or, Devotions and Exercises for the month of May. 2s.

A Devout Exercise in Honour of the Blessed Virgin
   Mary. From the Psalter and Prayers of S.
   Bonaventure. In Latin and English, with Indul-
   gences applicable to the Holy Souls. 32mo. 1s.
The Definition of the Immaculate Conception. 6d.
The Little Office of the Immaculate Conception. In
   Latin and English. By the Very Rev. Dr. Hu-
   senbeth. 32mo. 4d.; cloth, 6d.; roan, 1s.; calf or
   morocco, 2s. 6d.
The Little Office of the Immaculate Conception. In
   Latin and English. Translation approved of by
   the Bishop of Clifton. 3d.; or 100 for 16s. 8d.
Life of Our Lady in Verse. Edited by C. E. Tame. 2s.
Our Lady's Lament, and the Lamentation of St.
   Mary Magdalene. Edited by C. E. Tame. 2s.
Archconfraternity of Our Lady of Angels. 1s. per 100.
Litany of Our Lady of Angels. 1s. per 100.
Concise Portrait of the Blessed Virgin. 1s. per 100.
Origin of the Blue Scapular. 1d.
Miraculous Prayer—August Queen of Angels. 1s. 100.

Prayer-Books.

Washbourne's Edition of the "Garden of the Soul," in
   medium-sized type (small type as a rule being
   avoided). *For prices see page* 5.
The Little Garden. 6d., and upwards. *See page* 5.
Garden of the Soul. *Very large type*, 1s.; with E. & G.,
   1s. 6d.; French morocco, 2s. 6d.; with E. & G.,
   3s. 6d.; or superior edition, without E. & G.,
   3s. 6d.; morocco, turn over edges, 7s. 6d.
   Epistles and Gospels, in a separate volume, 2s.
Key of Heaven. *Very large type*, 1s. Leather 2s. 6d. gilt, 3s.
Catholic Piety; or, Key of Heaven. 32mo. 6d.;
   French morocco, 1s.; Velvet, 2s. 6d.; with
   E. & G., roan, 1s.; French morocco, 1s. 6d.;
   with rims, 2s.; French morocco, extra gilt, 2s.;
   Persian, 2s. 6d.; imitation ivory, with rims, 3s.;
   morocco, 3s. 6d.; velvet, with rims, 3s. 6d.
Manual of Catholic Piety. Edition with green border.
   French morocco, 2s. 6d.; morocco, 4s.

Holy Childhood. A book of simple Prayers and Instructions for very little children. 32mo., 1s.; gilt, 1s. 6d.

Catholic Piety, or Key of Heaven, with Epistles and Gospels. Large 32mo., roan, 1s. 6d. and 2s.; French morocco, with rims, 2s. 6d.; extra gilt, 3s.; with rims, 3s. 6d.; velvet, 3s. 6d. and 10s.

The Lily of St. Joseph; a little Manual of Prayers and Hymns for Mass. Price 2d.; cloth, 3d.; or with gilt lettering, 4d.; more strongly bound, 6d.; or with gilt edges, 8d.; roan, 1s.; French morocco, 1s. 6d.; calf, or morocco, 2s.; gilt, 2s. 6d.

"A prayer-book for children, which is not a childish book, a handy book for boys and girls, and for men and women too, if they wish for a short, easy-to-read, and devotional [prayer-book."— *Catholic Opinion.* It will be found very useful for children and for travellers."—*Weekly Register.* "A neat little compilation, which will be specially useful to our Catholic School-children. The hymns it contains are some of Fr. Faber's best."—*Universe.*

Devotions for Public and Private Use at the Way of the Cross. By Sister M. F. Clare. Illustrated, 1s.; red edges, 1s. 6d.

S. Patrick's Manual. By Sister M. F. Clare. 3s. 6d.

Path to Paradise. 3d. With 50 Illustrations, cloth, 4d.; superior paper, 6d.; with rims and clasp, 1s.

Manual of Catholic Devotion. 6d.; with Epistles and Gospels, 1s.; roan, with tuck, 1s. 6d.; calf or morocco, 2s. 6d.; imitation ivory, 2s. 6d.

S. Angela's Manual; a book of devout Prayers and Exercises for Female Youth. 16mo., cloth, red edges, 2s.; Persian, 3s. 6d.; calf, 4s. 6d.

Crown of Jesus. Persian calf, 6s.; calf or morocco, 7s. 6d. and 8s. 6d., with rims, 10s. 6d.; with turnover edges, 10s. 6d.; morocco, extra gilt, 10s. 6d., with rims, 12s. 6d.; ivory, with rims, 21s., 25s., 27s. 6d. and 30s.

The Little Prayer-Book for Ordinary Catholic Devotions. Cloth, 3d.

Catholic Hours: a Manual of Prayer, including Mass and Vespers. By J. R. Digby Beste, Esq. 32mo. cloth, 2s; red edges, 2s. 6d.; roan, 3s.; morocco, 6s.

Ursuline Manual. Persian calf, 7s. 6d.; morocco, 10s.

Missal (complete). Persian, 8s. 6d.; calf or morocco, 10s. 6d., with rims, 13s. 6d.; calf or morocco, extra gilt, 12s. 6d., with rims, 15s. 6d.; morocco, with turn-over edges, 13s. 6d.; morocco antique, 15s.; morocco, with two patent clasps, 20s.; russia antique, 20s.; velvet, with rims, 20s.; ivory, with rims, 31s. 6d.; morocco, with gilt mounts, with engravings, and in morocco case, £5.

Missal and Vesper Book. In one volume, morocco, 6s.; with clasp, 8s.

A Prayer to be said for three days before Holy Communion, and another for three days after. 1d., or 6s. 100.

A New Year's Gift to our Heavenly Father. 4d.

Occasional Prayers for Festivals. By Rev. T. Barge. 32mo. 4d. and 6d.; gilt, 1s.

Illustrated Manual of Prayers. 32mo. 3d.; cloth, 4d.

The Mass: and a devout method of assisting at it. From the French of M. Tronson. 4d.

Devotions for Mass. Very large type, 2d.

Memorare Mass. By the Poor Clares of Kenmare, 2d.

Fourteen Stations of the Holy Way of the Cross. By St. Liguori. Large type edition, 1d.

Indulgences attached to Medals, Crosses, Statues, &c., by the Blessing of His Holiness and of those privileged to give his Blessing. 1s. 2d. per 100, post free.

A Union of our life with the Passion of our Lord by a daily offering. 1s. 2d. per 100, post free.

Prayer for one's Confessor. 1s. 2d. per 100, post free.

Prayer to S. Philip Neri. 1d. each, or 6d. a dozen.

Litany of Resignation. 1s. 2d. per 100, post free.

A Christmas Offering. 1s. a 100, or 7s. 6d. a 1000.

Intentions for Indulgences. 7d. per 100, post free.

Catholic Psalmist: or, Manual of Sacred Music, with the Gregorian Chants for High Mass, Holy Week, &c. Compiled by C. B. Lyons, 4s.

The Complete Hymn Book, 136 Hymns. Price 1d.

Douai Bible. 2s. 6d.; Persian calf, 5s.; calf or morocco, 7s.; gilt, 8s. 6d.

New Testament, Notes and References, Large 4to., 7s. 6d.; small 8vo., 2s. 6d.

Church Hymns. By J. R. Digby Beste, Esq. 6d.

Catholic Choir Manual : Vespers, Hymns and Litanies, &c. Compiled by C. B. Lyons. 1s.

Burial of the Dead (Adults and Infants) in Latin and English. Royal 32mo. cloth, 6d. ; roan, 1s. 6d.

"Being in a portable form, will be found useful by those who are called upon to assist at that solemn rite."—*Tablet.*

Prayers for the Dying. 1s. 2d. per 100, post free.

Indulgenced Prayer before a Crucifix. 1d. ea., or 6s. 100.

Indulgenced Prayers for Souls in Purgatory. 1s. per 100.

Indulgenced Prayers for the Rosary for the Holy Souls. 1d. each, 6d. a dozen, 3s. per 100.

The Rosary for the Souls in Purgatory, *with Indulgenced Prayer.* 6d., 8d. and 9d. each. Medals separately, 1d. each, 9s. gross.

Rome, &c.

The History of the Italian Revolution. The Revolution of the Barricades. (1796—1849.) By the Chevalier O'Clery, M.P., K.S.G. 8vo. 7s. 6d.

Two Years in the Pontifical Zouaves. By Joseph Powell, Z.P. With 4 Engravings. 8vo. 3s. 6d.

"It affords us much pleasure, and deserves the notice of the Catholic public."—*Tablet.* "Familiar names meet the eye on every page, and as few Catholic circles in either country have not had a friend or relative at one time or another serving in the Pontifical Zouaves, the history of the formation of the corps, of the gallant youths, their sufferings, and their troubles, will be valued as something more than a contribution to modern Roman history."—*Freeman's Journal.*

The Victories of Rome. By Rev. Fr. Beste. 1s.

Rome and her Captors. Letters collected and edited by Count Henri d'Ideville, and translated by F. R. Wegg-Prosser. Cr. 8vo. 4s.

The Pope of Rome and the Popes of the Oriental Orthodox Church. By the Rev. Cæsarius Tondini, Barnabite. Second edition. 3s. 6d.

Defence of the Roman Church against Fr. Gratry. By Dom Gueranger. 1s. 6d.

Personal Recollections of Rome. By W. J. Jacob, Esq., late of the Pontifical Zouaves. 8vo. 1s. 6d.

The Roman Question. By F. C. Husenbeth, D.D. 6d.
Supremacy of the Roman See. By C. E. Tame. 6d.
Rome: Present, Past, and Future. By Rev. Dr. M'Corry. 6d.
The Rule of the Pope-King. By Rev. Fr. Martin. 6d.
The Years of Peter. By an Ex-Papal Zouave. 1d.
The Catechism of the Council. By a D.C.L. 2d.
Civilization and the See of Rome. By Lord Robert Montagu, M.P. 6d.
Rome, semper eadem. By D. P. M.O'Mahony. 1s. 6d.
A Few Remarks on a pamphlet entitled the "Divine Decrees." 6d.

Tales, or Books for the Library.

Bessy; or the Fatal Consequence of Telling Lies. By the writer of "The Rat Pond, or the Effects of Disobedience." 1s.; stronger bound, 1s. 6d.; gilt, 2s.
Stories for my Children.—The Angels and the Sacraments. Square 16mo. 1s.
Canon Schmid's Tales, selected from his works. New translation, with Original Illustrations, 3s. 6d. Separately: Canary Bird, 6d.; Dove, 6d.; Inundation, 6d. Rose Tree, 6d.; Water Jug, 6d.; Wooden Cross, 6d.
Tom's Crucifix, and other Tales. By M. F. S. 3s.
"Eight simple stories for the use of teachers of Christian doctrine."—*Universe.* "This is a volume of short, plain, and simple stories, written with the view of illustrating the Catholic religion practically by putting Catholic practices in an interesting light before the mental eyes of children. The whole of the tales in the volume before us are exceedingly well written."—*Register.*

Catherine Hamilton. By the author of "Tom's Crucifix," &c. Fcap. 8vo. 2s. 6d.; gilt, 3s.
Catherine grown Older. Fcap. 8vo. 2s. 6d.; gilt 3s.
Simple Tales. Square 16mo. cloth antique, 2s. 6d.
"Contains five pretty stories of a true Catholic tone, interspersed with some short pieces of poetry. . . Are very affecting, and told in such a way as to engage the attention of any child."—*Register.* "This is a little book which we can recommend with great confidence. The tales are simple, beautiful, and pathetic."—*Catholic Opinion.* "It belongs to a class of books of which the want is generally much felt by Catholic parents."—*Dublin Review.* "Beautifully written. 'Little Terence' is a gem of a Tale."—*Tablet.*

Terry O'Flinn's Examination of Conscience. By the Very Rev. Dr. Tandy. Fcap. 8vo. 1s. 6d.; extra gilt, 2s.; cheap edition, 1s.

"The writer possesses considerable literary power."—*Register*.

The Adventures of a Protestant in Search of a Religion: being the Story of a late Student of Divinity at Bunyan Baptist College; a Nonconformist Minister, who seceded to the Catholic Church. By Iota. 5s.; cheap edition, 3s.

"Will well repay its perusal."—*Universe*. "This precious volume."—*Baptist*. "No one will deny 'Iota' the merit of entire originality."—*Civilian*. "A valuable addition to every Catholic library." *Tablet*. "There is much cleverness in it."—*Nonconformist*. "Malicious and wicked."—*English Independent*.

The People's Martyr, a Legend of Canterbury. 4s.

Rupert Aubray. By the Rev. T. J. Potter. 3s.

Percy Grange. By the same author. 3s.

Farleyes of Farleye. By the same author. 2s. 6d.

Sir Humphrey's Trial. By the same author. 2s. 6d.

Fairy Tales for Little Children. By Madeleine Howley Meehan. Fcap. 1s.; cloth extra, 1s. 6d.; gilt, 2s.

"Full of imagination and dreams, and at the same time with excellent point and practical aim, within the reach of the intelligence of infants."—*Universe*. "Pleasing, simple stories, combining instruction with amusement."—*Register*.

Rosalie; or, the Memoirs of a French Child. Written by herself. Fcap. 8vo., 1s. and 1s. 6d.; extra gilt, 2s.

"It is prettily told, and in a natural manner. The account of Rosalie's illness and First Communion is very well related. We can recommend the book for the reading of children."—*Tablet*. "The tenth chapter is beautiful."—*Universe*.

The Story of Marie and other Tales. Fcap. 8vo., 2s.; gilt, 3s.; or separately:—The Story of Marie, 2d.; Nelly Blane, and A Contrast, 2d.; A Conversion and a Death-Bed, 2d.; Herbert Montagu, 2d.; Jane Murphy, The Dying Gipsy, and The Nameless Grave, 2d.; The Beggars, and True and False Riches, 2d.; Pat and his Friend, 2d.

"A very nice little collection of stories, thoroughly Catholic in their teaching."—*Tablet*. "A series of short pretty stories, told with much simplicity."—*Universe*. "A number of short pretty stories, replete with religious teaching, told in simple language."—*Weekly Register*.

Sir Ælfric and other Tales. By the Rev. G. Bampfield. 18mo. 6d.; cloth, 1s.; gilt, 1s. 6d.

The Last of the Catholic O'Malleys. A Tale. By M. Taunton. 18mo. cloth, 1s. 6d.; extra, 2s.

"A sad and stirring tale, simply written, and sure to secure for itself readers."—*Tablet.* "Deeply interesting. It is well adapted for parochial and school libraries."—*Weekly Register.* "A very pleasing tale."—*The Month.*

Eagle and Dove. From the French of Mademoiselle Zénaïde Fleuriot. By Emily Bowles. Cr. 8vo., 5s.

"We recommend our readers to peruse this well-written story."—*Register.* "One of the very best stories we have ever dipped into."—*Church Times.* "Admirable in tone and purpose."—*Church Herald.* "A real gain. It possesses merits far above the pretty fictions got up by English writers."—*Dublin Review.* "There is an air of truth and sobriety about this little volume, nor is there any attempt at sensation."—*Tablet.*

Cistercian Legends of the 13th Century. Translated from the Latin by the Rev. Henry Collins. 3s.

Cloister Legends: or, Convents and Monasteries in the Olden Time. *Second Edition.* Cr. 8vo. 4s.

Chats about the Rosary; or, Aunt Margaret's Little Neighbours. Fcap. 8vo. 3s.

"There is scarcely any devotion so calculated as the Rosary to keep up a taste for piety in little children, and we must be grateful for any help in applying its lessons to the daily life of those who already love it in their unconscious tribute to its value and beauty."—*Month.* "We do not know of a better book for reading aloud to children, it will teach them to understand and to love the Rosary."—*Tablet.* Illustrative of each of the mysteries, and connecting each with the practice of some particular virtue."—*Catholic Opinion.*

Margarethe Verflassen. Translated from the German by Mrs. Smith Sligo. Fcap. 8vo. 3s.; gilt, 3s. 6d.

"A portrait of a very holy and noble soul, whose life was passed in constant practical acts of the love of God."—*Weekly Register.* "It is the picture of a true woman's life, well fitted up with the practice of ascetic devotion and loving unwearied activity about all the works of mercy."—*Tablet.*

Keighley Hall and other Tales. By Elizabeth King. 18mo. 6d.; cloth, 1s.; 1s. 6d.; gilt, 2s.

Ned Rusheen. By the Poor Clares. Crown 8vo. 6s.

The Prussian Spy. A Novel. By V. Valmont. 4s.

Sir Thomas Maxwell and his Ward. By Miss Bridges. Fcap. 8vo. 2s.

Adolphus; or, the Good Son. 18mo. gilt, 6d.

Nicholas; or, the Reward of a Good Action. 6d.

The Lost Children of Mount St. Bernard. Gilt, 6d.

The Baker's Boy; or, the Results of Industry. 6d.
A Broken Chain. 18mo. gilt, 6d.
The Truce of God: a Tale of the Eleventh Century. By G. H. Miles. 4s.
Tales and Sketches. By Charles Fleet. 8vo. cloth, 2s. and 2s. 6d.; cloth, gilt, 3s. 6d.
The Artist of Collingwood. By Baron Na Carriag. 3s. 6d.; cheap edition, 2s.
The Convent Prize Book. By the author of "Geraldine." Fcap. 8vo. 2s. 6d.; gilt, 3s. 6d.
Munster Firesides; or, the Barrys of Beigh. By E. Hall. 3s. 6d.
The Village Lily. Fcap. 8vo. 1s.; gilt, 1s. 6d.
Forty Years of American Life. By Dr. Nichols. 5s.
The Journey of Sophia and Eulalie to the Palace of True Happiness. Translated by the Rev. Father Bradbury, Mount St. Bernard's. Fcap. 8vo. 3s. 6d.; cheap edition, 2s. 6d.
The Fisherman's Daughter. By Conscience. 4s.
The Amulet. By Hendrick Conscience. 4s.
Count Hugo of Graenhove. By Conscience. 4s.
The Village Innkeeper. By Conscience. 4s.
Happiness of being Rich. By Conscience. 4s.
Ludovic and Gertrude. By Conscience. 4s.
The Young Doctor. By Conscience. 4s.
Margaret Roper. By A. M. Stewart. 6s., gilt, 7s.
Florence O'Neill. By A. M. Stewart. 5s. and 6s.
Limerick Veteran. By the same. 5s. and 6s.
Life in the Cloister. By the same. 3s. 6d.
Alone in the World. By the same. 4s. 6d.
Festival Tales. By J. F. Waller. 5s.
My Dream; and Verses Miscellaneous. By Wallace Herbert. With a frontispiece. 12mo., 5s.
Poems. By H. N. Oxenham. *Third Edition.* 3s. 6d.
The Continental Fish Cook; or, a Few Hints on Maigre Dinners. By M. J. N. de Frederic. 18mo. 1s.
Certain Difficulties felt by Anglicans. Letters to Dr. Pusey and the Duke of Norfolk. By V. Rev. Dr. Newman. 5s. 6d.

Educational and Miscellaneous.

Horace. Literally translated by Smart. 2s.
Virgil. Literally translated by Davidson. 2s. 6d.
History of Modern Europe. With Preface by Bishop Weathers. cloth, 5s. ; roan, 5s. 6d.; gilt, 6s.
Burton's Ecclesiastical History. 1s.
Biographical Readings. By A. M. Stewart. 4s. 6d.
General Questions in History, Chronology, Geography, the Arts, &c. By A. M. Stewart. 4s. 6d.
University Education ; or, Monastic Studies. By a Monk of St. Augustine's, Ramsgate. 8vo. 2s. 6d.
Elements of Philosophy, comprising Logic, and General Principles of Metaphysics. By Rev. W. H. Hill, S.J. Second edition, 8vo. 6s.
Catechism of the History of England. Cloth, 1s.
History of Ireland. By T. Young. 18mo. cloth, 2s. 6d.
History of Ireland. By Miss Cusack. Illustrated. 11s.
The Patriots' History of Ireland. By Miss Cusack. 2s. ; cloth gilt, 2s. 6d.
Ireland Ninety Years Ago. 12mo., 1s.
A Chronological Sketch of the Kings of England and France. With Anecdotes. By H. Murray Lane. 2s. 6d. ; or England, 1s. 6d., France, 1s. 6d.

"Admirably adapted for teaching young children the elements of English and French history."—*Tablet.* "A very useful little publication."—*Weekly Register.* "An admirably arranged little work for the use of children."—*Universe.*

Extracts from the Fathers and other Writers of the Church. 12mo. cloth, 4s. 6d.
Brickley's Standard Table Book, ½d.
Washbourne's Multiplication Table on a sheet, 3s. per 100. Specimen sent for 1d. stamp.
Easy Lessons: or, Self-Instruction in Irish. By Rev. Ulick J. Bourke. 12mo., 3s. 6d.
The Catholic Alphabet of Scripture Subjects. Price, on a sheet, plain, 1s.; coloured, 2s.; mounted on linen, to fold in a case, 3s. 6d. ; varnished, on linen, on rollers, 4s.
Book of Family Crests and Mottos. Upwards of four thousand engravings. 2 vols., cr. 8vo., 24s.

Culpepper. Brook's Family Herbal. Coloured Engravings. 5s. 6d.; plain, 3s. 6d.
Bell's Modern Reader and Speaker. Cloth, 3s. 6d.
Cogery's Third French Course, with Vocabulary. 2s.

Music (*Net*).

BY HERR WILHELM SCHULTHES.

Veni Domine. Motett for Four Voices. 2s.; vocal, 6d.
Cor Jesu, Salus in Te Sperantium. 2s.; with harp accompaniment, 2s. 6d.; abridged edition, 3d.
Mass of the Holy Child Jesus, and Ave Maria for unison and congregational singing, with organ accompaniment. 3s. Vocal Part, 4d.; cloth, 6d.
The Ave Maria of this Mass can be had for Four Voices, with the Ingressus Angelus. 1s. 3d.
Recordare. Oratio Jeremiæ Prophetæ. 1s.
Ne projicias me a facie Tua. Motett for Four Voices. (T.B.) 1s. 3d.
Benediction Service, with 36 Litanies. 6s.
Oratory Hymns. 2 vols., 8s.
Regina Cœli. Motett for Four Voices. 3s.; vocal, 1s.
Twelve Latin Hymns, for Vespers, &c. 2s.

Catholic Hymnal. English Words. For Children, Church, Convent, Confraternity and Catholic Family Use. For one, two, or four voices, with accompaniment. By Leopold de Prins. 4to., 2s., bound, 3s.

"Simple and effective. Once the Hymnal becomes known, it is sure to become popular."—*Freeman's Journal.*

Six Litany Chants. By F. Leslie. 6d.
Litanies. By Rev. J. McCarthy. 1s. 3d.
The Elements of Gregorian or Plain Chant and Modern Music. 2s. 6d.
Portfolio. With a patent metallic back. 3s.

A separate Catalogue of **FOREIGN Books, Educational Books, Books for the Library or for Prizes; School and General Stationery, Secondhand Books, and Crucifixes and other Religious Articles.**

R. Washbourne, 18 Paternoster Row, London.

INDEX TO AUTHORS.

Author	Page	Author	Page
Arnold, Miss M. J.	19	Husenbeth, Dr.	2, 18, 20, 21, 22
A'Kempis, Thomas	10	Kenny, Dr.	17
Allies, T. W., Esq.	12	King, Miss	28
Amherst, Bishop	7	Laing, Rev. Dr.	14, 17, 21
Bagshawe, Rev. J. B.	15, 16	Lane, H. Murray, Esq.	30
Bampfield, Rev. G.	27	M'Corry, Rev. Dr.	17, 26
Barge, Rev. T.	24	Macdaniel, Miss	6, 21
Beste, J. R. D., Esq.	12, 23, 25	Macleod, Rev. X. D.	21
Beste, Rev. K. D.	25	Manning, Most Rev. Dr.	15, 20
Bethell, Rev. A. P.	21	Marshall, T. W. M., Esq.	11
Blosius	8	Meehan, Madeleine Howley	27
Bona, Cardinal	8	Mermillod, Mgr.	9
Boudon, Mgr.	8	Milner, Bishop	6
Bowles, Emily	28	M. F. S.	2, 19, 26
Bradbury, Rev. Fr.	29	Nary, Rev. J.	15
Browne, F. G. K.	15	Newman, Dr.	2
Brownlow, Rev. W. R. B.	7, 14	O'Clery, Chevalier	25
Burder, Rt. Rev. Abbot	7, 8	O'Mahony, D. P. M.	26
Burke, S. H., M.A.	13	Oratorian Lives of the Saints	18
Butler, Alban	9, 18	Oxenham, H. N.	13, 29
Challoner, Bishop	17, 20	Ozanam, Professor	12
Collins, Rev. Fr.	9, 10	Philpin, Rev. Fr.	7
Compton, Herbert	3	Platus, Fr. Jerome	17
Dechamps, Mgr.	12	Poirier, Bishop	16
Deham, Rev. A.	6	Poor Clares	14, 20, 23
Dixon, Rev. Fr.	1, 18	Powell, J., Esq.	25
Doyle, Canon	2	Prins, Leopold de	31
Doyotte, Rev. Père	6	Pye, H. J., Esq.	17
Dupanloup, Mgr.	9, 17	Ravignan, Père	9
Francis of Sales, St.	12, 13	Redmond, Rev. Dr.	14
Frassinetti	16	Richardson, Rev. Fr.	17
Gibson, Rev. H.	15	Rowley, Fr. A. J.	2
Grace Ramsay	20	Schulthes, Herr	31
Gracian, Fr. Baltasar	3	Shakespeare	29
Grant, Bishop	6	Sligo, A. V. Smith, Esq.	19
Gueranger	25	Sligo, Mrs. Smith	28
Hedley, Bishop	14	Stewart, A. M.	23, 29, 30
Henry, Lucien	8	Tame, C. E., Esq.	22, 26
Herbert, Lady	8, 9, 19	Tandy, Very Rev. Dr.	27
Hervey, Mrs. T. K.	1	Taunton, Mrs.	28
Hill, Rev. Fr.	30	Tondini, Rev. C.	9, 25
Hope, Mrs.	10	Wegg-Prosser, F. R.	25
Humphrey, Rev. Fr., S.J.	1	Williams, Canon	17

CONTENTS.

	Page		Page
New Books	1	Our Lady, Works relating to	21
The Sacred Heart & St. Joseph	6	Prayer-Books	22
Religious Reading	7	Rome, &c.	25
Religious Instruction	15	Tales, or Books for Library	26
Dramas, Comedies, Farces	18	Educational Works	30
Lives of Saints, &c.	18	Music	31

www.ingramcontent.com/pod-product-compliance
Lightning Source LLC
Chambersburg PA
CBHW031449160426
43195CB00010BB/919